Trauma-Sensitive Theology

Trauma-Sensitive Theology

Thinking Theologically in the Era of Trauma

Jennifer Baldwin

CASCADE *Books* · Eugene, Oregon

TRAUMA-SENSITIVE THEOLOGY
Thinking Theologically in the Era of Trauma

Cascade Books
An Imprint of Wipf and Stock Publishers
199 W. 8th Ave., Suite 3
Eugene, OR 97401

www.wipfandstock.com

PAPERBACK ISBN: 978-1-4982-9684-7
HARDCOVER ISBN: 978-1-5326-4312-5
EBOOK ISBN: 978-1-5326-4313-2

Cataloguing-in-Publication data:
_____

Names: Baldwin, Jennifer, author.
Title: Trauma-sensitive theology : thinking theologically in the era of trauma / Jennifer Baldwin.
Description: Eugene, OR : Cascade Books, 2018 | Includes bibliographical references.
Identifiers: ISBN 978-1-4982-9684-7 (paperback) | ISBN 978-1-5326-4312-5 (hardcover) | ISBN 978-1-5326-4313-2 (ebook)
Subjects: LCSH: Psychic trauma—Religious aspects—Christianity. | Post-traumatic stress disorder—Religious aspects—Christianity. | Post-traumatic stress disorder—Patients—Religious life. | Spiritual healing. | Psychology, Religious.
Classification: BV4910.45 .B35 2018 (print) | BV4910.45 .B35 (ebook)
_____

Manufactured in the U.S.A.   SEPTEMBER 18, 2018

To those who survive,
Those who offer compassionate and wise care,
And those whose love and support sustains.

Table of Contents

Acknowledgments

Writing a monograph is a labor of love. The labor of love is not only the work of the author; it is shared by those who support and nurture the work along the way. I desire to express my sincere gratitude to those who have travelled with me along the journey of constructing a trauma-sensitive theology: Antje Jackelén, Richard F. Wilson, Monica Coleman, Vitor Westhelle, and Lea Schweitz. This work is a blending of my theological and clinical work. I am forever grateful for the community of Internal Family Systems including trainers and learning partners in this remarkable model: Susan McConnell, Terrilee Dalton, Arlene Brennan, Mary Steege, Beth O'Neil, and Richard Schwartz for developing the model. Thank you to my movement communities for offering space to connect with moving wisdom: Susan Cahill, Marlo Fisken, Heidi Coker, authentic movement group partners, the 5 Rhythms community in Atlanta, and the tap, pole, and aerial dance communities. Elonda Clay, thank you for being my academic partner-in-crime, ever present source of encouragement, and creative instigator. Your friendship has been a gift, your conversation always enlightening and encouraging, and your collegiality a source of inspiration and motivation. Carol Schickel, thank you for your support through all of the ups and downs of academic work, helpful and thoughtful reading of this text, clinical mentorship that has contributed to who I am as a therapist, and your encouragement and compassion.

To my clients and the community of survivors, your resiliency continues to remind me of the tremendous strength that dwells within. You are who I do theological work on behalf of. I only hope this book reflects my deep respect, desire to honor your experience, and demonstrate my deep abiding faith in hope and resiliency, especially in the darkest of nights. Thank you to my family who has extended love to me and who have contributed to making me the person I am. Lynn Crawford, thank you for listening and supporting as I worked my way through roadblocks, and for your reading of this manuscript. My gratitude to Nick Cappello, my partner, who graciously gave up many weekends of companionship to support the writing of this work and made sure I never went hungry. Finally, thank you to Charlie Collier and the staff of Cascade Books for your faith in this work and patience in its reception.

Introduction

Moving towards a Trauma-Sensitive Theology

WHAT IS TRAUMA-SENSITIVE THEOLOGY?

For centuries the church has been a place of faith, community, hope, ritual practice, and support during experiences of loss and grief. Religious faith across traditions fundamentally seeks to provide people with a way of understanding the world and their experiences within it. Questions such as "How did human beings come to be?," "What is our place in this world?," and "How do I make enough sense of suffering to be able to continue?" are some of the key existential concerns which religious faith and practice has sought to answer with the best knowledge available at the time. Of course, as time progresses we learn more and more, and the answers that made sense of the world in 1000 BCE are different than the answers that make sense in 33 CE or 2020 CE. The ability and mandate to allow religious thinking and practice to mature is at the heart of healthy and wise religious practice. It is one of the key hallmarks of the Reformation era within Christianity. Christian faith, confession, and practice must continue to mature in order to resist stagnation and static adherence that calcifies into the kinds of rigid religiosity that understandably fall prey to accusations of irrelevance, dogmatism, pathogensis. Likewise, we must have the courage, confidence, and clarity to re/form our theology and liturgy so that it continues to make use of the best knowledge of our time for the benefit, growth, and health of individuals, communities, and society. Making use of the best knowledge of our time—whether that be the insights of astrophysics, evolution, psychology, economics, or politics—doesn't mean that we have to abandon the narratives of faith that support our meaning making. However, it does require us to venture beyond our safe familiarity in order to meet the present needs and understandings of our world.

Trauma-Sensitive Theology is a venture into a re/formation of Christian theology and practice with the intention of honoring the stories of faith that have nourished past generations while infusing those narratives with the wisdoms of contemporary knowledge in order to meet the variety of needs of persons and communities struggling under the burden of traumatic experience/s and response.

THE IMPETUS FOR CONSTRUCTING TRAUMA-SENSITIVE THEOLOGY

In one sense, the phrase Trauma-Sensitive Theology emerged during the dissertation phase of my doctoral work in systematic theology with an emphasis in religion and science. It developed over the process of engaging in clinical practice as a psychotherapist, exploring the area of trauma studies, traumatology, as a researcher, attuning to the rhythms of congregational life as a clergy person, and reflecting on the role of the divine and religion in our lives as a systematic constructive theologian. In another sense, Trauma-Sensitive Theology reflects my own journey as a person of faith attempting to find a way through trauma. It is a journey that far too many of us, especially women and persons of color, travel. While the particular stories of our encounters with violence differ, the process of recovering from encounters that overwhelm us are similar. When it comes to how we, as a society, as communities of faith/s, and as individuals, understand and talk about trauma, I don't get to sit on the side lines; talking about trauma is not theoretical in my life, it is one of the primary stories of my life. So, I come to this book as much as a survivor of trauma as I do a theologian or mental health clinician.

My position as survivor, clergy, theologian, and clinician are essentially formative and informative for this work. It is difficult to parse out which part of my larger self is any more engaged than the others since all of those parts of me bring a distinctive fundamental commitment to this work. My survivor part is insistent that survivors of trauma are respected, honored, and have the required space for restoration from traumatic injury. Survivors are not shattered, annihilated, nor "existentially undone" as other theologians have named them to be. Survivors are wounded, resilient, burdened, wise, challenged, fearful, courageous, and persistent. As a survivor of trauma, I have felt the crushing weight of traumatic responses—nightmares, flashbacks, numbing, hypervigilance, difficulty trusting, craving safety. At times, I have felt broken or shattered; though, I also learned that *feeling* and *being* are different things. I have felt spoiled and given my whole being to Christianity, God, and Jesus as a way of becoming clean again. I have felt God's promises seemingly crumble under the force of post-traumatic response. And, I have found a more expansive path for honoring the vivifying power of the divine in all. Being a survivor of trauma and a person of faith are not mutually exclusive and faith does not exclude one from or prevent post-traumatic responses. Actually, I am a survivor of traumatic experience and a survivor of post-traumatic response.

As clergy and a person of faith who has survived trauma and post-traumatic response, I have a commitment of speaking on behalf of and for the benefit of communities of faith. My relationship with the church began in high school, shortly after the death of my paternal grandmother. I was a freshman when she died suddenly (from my vantage point). I remember attending her funeral, holding back tears, then reading the Bible out of my own need for the first time. I clumsily found my way to the Psalms and found comfort and a feeling of security. A month after her funeral, as a good Baptist raised in the South, I gave my life to Christ and started attending church with fierce devotion that continued throughout high school, college, numerous mission trips, and Bible study and youth group leadership. During my late teens through mid-twenties, I loved God and the church without hesitation or competition. Of course, communities of faith are never perfect and I encountered several glimpses into the destructive dimensions of congregational life in church leadership. I was called into a "heresy trial" in the last month as youth minister of a small conservative Presbyterian church (PCA) for indicating that I wanted to learn from a leading Old Testament Theologian at a Presbyterian (PCUSA) seminary. I saw a senior pastor driven almost to the brink of insanity following a budget crisis that turned personal and threatened to render him swiftly homeless and unemployed. I know that the church can be a place of harm as well as a place of support and health. When it comes to the care offered to survivors of trauma, the church, in its ignorance of traumatic processing, is too often a place of misunderstanding and re-traumatization.

My personal identity as a theologian was cultivated through and in spite of my adolescent religious experience. As theologian Paul Tillich points out, robust and healthy faith must include within itself the experience of doubt. Without doubt, the particular content of faith fails to grow into maturity. My early theological mind was seeded in high school and

3

took root in college. During my college years, I fell in love with theology. I found theological discourse, as I encountered it, engaging, robust, evocative, and supportive. At that time, I loved the way theologians like Karl Barth, Paul Tillich, James Cone, Mary Daly, Stanley Hauerwas, Leonardo Boff and others took their lived experiences and the needs of the society and community seriously. They all, in their own ways, struggled with experiences and consequences of violence and sought to speak of God and faith in a way that honored human and environmental struggle. This was the theology that I loved; it was the theology I wanted to do. I remember sitting down to write a systematic theology as I understood faith at that juncture of life—and only getting a few paragraphs into the introduction.

Of course, the theological musings of a 21 year old are often immature, over simplified, and idealistic—at least mine were. In my senior year, I had a profound crisis of faith in which I felt like God had lied to me. I had had the belief that if I "gave everything" to God that he would lift the shame and burden of trauma from me. When post-traumatic response finally showed up full force, my mid-adolescent self could only conclude that God had betrayed me. I was sincerely willing to die on the mission field if that was God's will; yet, instead I was in an immediately failing marriage, hovering at the poverty line, and felt trapped. During this time, I was drawn to Holocaust or Shoah theological writings and memoirs—Elie Wiesel, Primo Levi, Viktor Frankel, and others. It was these stories of profound trauma and survival only by the slimmest of margins that gave me a "safe enough" place to explore trauma. I could not process my own experiences of trauma in my childhood and early adolescence or the ways in which my marriage was emotionally abusive; but I could empathetically hear and hold the narratives of others who found a way to survive profound trauma. Their survival and wrestling with the God of their faith gave me permission to reengage and reconstruct my understanding of God.

Post-traumatic response hit full force when I moved to Chicago for doctoral work in Systematic Theology with an emphasis in Religion and Science. The move to Chicago was both a move away from all of my social supports and a decision to end my marriage. For the first year of my doctoral studies, I struggled with flashbacks, nightmares, dissociation, I juggled my personal struggles that felt like they would drown me with the need to adequately perform the part of the smart and capable doctoral student. During the day, I performed the part of doctoral student of theology and at night I participated in and moderated an online community of trauma survivors. I heard stories and supported survivors through debilitating traumatic responses, significant self injury impulses and actions, lures towards suicide, and relationship failures. I also heard story after story of the ways in which their religious leaders, who were so inept in their understanding of trauma, counseled them to pray harder in order to end flashbacks, took their continuing struggle through traumatic processing as a sign of a lack of faith in God, misunderstood self-medication or self injury as a moral failing, or simply wrote them off as hopelessly shattered. These failures of the church only added to survivor's struggle to survive post-traumatic response. Personally, at times, the struggle to navigate care for this online, global community of survivors, to perform the role of brilliant doctoral student, and cope with my own processing of divorce and trauma was overwhelming and I felt like I could barely continue reading giants in the field who felt so disconnected from my struggle and community of trauma survivors.

In an attempt to reconnect and reinvigorate my affection for theology, I explored what made those formative years as an undergraduate beginning theologian so captivating and invigorating—it was always the theologians commitment to communities of persons in the midst of struggle. Theology, for me, needed to matter to someone in the midst of their suffering. I realized that if a particular theological frame offered no assistance or comfort to someone in the dark nights of the soul at three in the early morning then it was not a theology that mattered to me. In that first year of doctoral work, as I was concluding my process for ordination, I vowed that the community from which and to whom I do theology would be, and continues to be, the ecclesia of trauma survivors. Trauma survivors are the community of witness that inform and guide how I evaluate theological constructions. If the god of a theological frame causes further injury or impedes the resiliency of survivors in the midst of post-traumatic response and process, then that god is not God for me. This commitment to trauma survivors, like any other foundational commitment (e.g., God's sovereignty, omnipotence, preferential option for the poor, siding with the oppressed, facilitation of patriarchy), of course, shapes all of theological loci of systematic theology and guides my further study.

I clarified my theological community in 2006, was ordained in 2007, and realized quickly after that if I were to take on the research area of trauma and theology and were teaching that I would likely be receiving disclosures of trauma from future students. In late 2005, I had disclosed some of my experiences to a professor and the experience, while intended to be supportive, was formative for how I did not want to respond to others. Hearing disclosures of traumatic experiences is a gift and requires tender skill. I knew that both my academic and clerical training were ill equipped in preparing me to respond the way I desired to persons who were disclosing trauma stories. I knew I needed training as a mental health clinician and I enrolled in a counseling psychology program while still in the midst of doctoral work.

My clinical training was a tremendous addition to my pastoral and theological training. It helped form me into a good general clinician; however, like most programs, it did not provide adequate education on trauma and traumatology. For some reason, courses in trauma are not required by nearly all states for licensure. This is disconcerting because many of the issues for which people seek therapy have roots in past traumatic experience. As a scholar, I quickly realized that I would need to supplement my graduate clinical education with professional trainings outside of the academic requirements. I joined professional societies, such as the International Society for the Study of Trauma and Dissociation, registered for intensive post-graduate clinical trainings in Internal Family Systems, EMDR, and hypnotherapy, and read everything I could find on traumatic process and related mental health concerns. As a clinician, I learn again and again how remarkable our systems are for coping with overwhelming experiences and pathways of resolution and resiliency. I am awestruck by our body's capacity to hold the wreckage of traumatic experience/s until the person is safe enough to process the experience/s.

Trauma-Sensitive Theology emerges out years of learnings in systematic theology and trauma informed psychotherapy and traumatology. It flows in the service of trauma survivors who are congregation members and clergy who desire to provide supportive, stabilizing, grace-filled presence to persons and communities impacted by trauma. Trauma-sensitive theology is a theoretical lens, ethical commitment, and guide for praxis that extends in most areas of pastoral care, practical theology, pastoral counseling, liturgy, homiletics, and care for souls, minds, and bodies. It is not limited to or excluded from clear lines of theological tradition and can be incorporated in the pastoral theology and praxis across theological traditions, including and not limited to the Reformed, Lutheran, Evangelical, Augustine, Anglican, Free Church traditions, and across the World Religions.

PRIMARY COMMITMENTS OF CONSTRUCTING A TRAUMA-SENSITIVE THEOLOGY

There are four primary commitments of Trauma-Sensitive Theology: the priority of bodily experience, full acceptance of trauma narratives, natural given-ness of human psychological multiplicity, and faith in the robust resiliency of trauma survivors. These four commitments are key for the construction of trauma-sensitive theology and corresponding pastoral care and presence. Additionally, they speak to some of the most challenging features of post-traumatic response for survivors. As commitments, these four elements run as a through line throughout the text as both the foundation and the criteria of assessment. If an element of constructive theology violates any of these four commitments, then that is a signal that more constructive work needs to be done.

The first commitment is the priority of bodily experience. Trauma is fundamentally a bodily experience. Trauma and the variety of trauma stress disorders, acute traumatic stress (ASD), post-traumatic stress (PTSD), and rape trauma syndrome (RTS), are classified as mental health/psychological concerns; however, traumatic response originates and is perpetuated in the body. Some experiences of trauma involve direct and fairly obvious violation of the body (e.g., sexual assault, car accidents, physical assaults, etc.); while others involve the body in less visible though also potent ways (e.g., alterations of hormone and neurochemical levels). Bessel van der Kolk, one of the global leading experts on traumatic stress, highlights and insists that the body retains the somatic memory of traumatic experiences either directly in tissue cells or indirectly through the body's natural changes in hormones that accompany fight or flight or dissociative escape responses. Our bodies respond to increases in adrenaline and cortisol (the escape and stress hormones) alternations in hormone levels are present at the time of the traumatic experience and are reinforced in post-traumatic responses of hyper- and hypo-arousal, including most of the symptoms of trauma response. The body's response in processing traumatic experience/s must be a component in building resiliency and promoting wellbeing. Trauma-oriented interventions that focus exclusively on the cognitive dimension of traumatic memory without corresponding care for the multiple ways in which the body holds traumatic response are doomed to be ineffective in the long run. Traumatic experiences cannot be processed solely by means of intellect or faith. Strategies for resolving the consequences of trauma must include the body.

For theologians and religious professionals, the importance of attending to the body presents a challenge. Most of our theological traditions, especially after the Enlightenment, place significant importance on human rationality. The mind, rationality, soul are all valued as more holy than the body, emotions, flesh. This dynamic plays out in theological systems that identify "rationality" or the mind as what makes human beings in the image of God, the naming of the body and intuitions emerging from the body as the "flesh" that is inherently sinful, and liturgical practices that reduce or eliminate the dignity of full human sensation in worship. Historically, the denigration of the body was the goal of the holy ascetic life; contemporarily, this practice morphs into the valorization of "thin-ness" in western culture and the idea that "thin" is healthy, nay "thin" is a mark of holiness. In terms of religious ethics, the naming of the body as unholy or less important than the spirit or mind has generated significant problems with regard to the promotion of consensual sex on one hand, and the justice-seeking denouncement of perpetrators of sexual violence and care for victims on the other. Christian faith, practice, and theology has a long way to go in overcoming the denigration of the body that has been a hallmark of the "good" or spiritual life. Prioritizing the body in trauma-sensitive reflection and practices is both a challenge to the predominant ways to do-ing and be-ing the church as well as an antidote for correcting the imbalances that emerge when we fail to connect to the body stories of our personal lives and the lives of those in our community and society. The church must work towards resurrecting the honor and wisdom of the physical body if it seeks to be a resource for vital, healthful lives and communities.

The second commitment of trauma-sensitive theology is acceptance of trauma narratives. One of the main reasons why individuals and communities do not share their experience/s of traumatic violation with those who could offer restorative support is the fear that their experiences will be questioned and/or not believed. Experiences of trauma are already, by definition, overwhelming to our systems of understanding and coping. Disclosing experiences of trauma to others is already difficult and, for some, terrifying. For too many, the courage to disclose trauma narratives is met with disbelief in the form of "survivor shaming," questions of "are you sure that's what happened?" or "but he's such a 'good' guy," and/or statements that directly challenge the disclosure. Survivors of traumatic interpersonal violence are especially vulnerable to the secondary injury of having their narratives discounted, overanalyzed, claimed as false, exaggerated, or manipulative. While law enforcement personnel have an added burden of responsibility with regard to "fact" finding when hearing narrative accounts of trauma and violation due to the current thresholds of "proof," those of us in care providing professions do survivors a tremendous disservice, if not injury, when our initial response to disclosures of trauma is to question. For clergy, pastoral care providers, mental health care providers, and lay support givers there is little value in initially responding to survivor disclosures with an intent to verify the narrative. Rather, the most helpful—even healing—response we can offer is to accept a survivor's trauma narrative as it is disclosed to us in that moment with a loosely held expectation that the narrative will shift as the experience/s continue to process. The role of religious care and mental health professionals is not to adjudicate the "facts" of trauma; it is to advocate for safety, to support and facilitate the repair of traumatic injury, and to promote recovery and resiliency. These aims can only happen if we accept narratives of traumatic experience/s as they are understood by the survivor of trauma.

The third primary commitment of trauma-sensitive theology is the natural given-ness of human psychological multiplicity. On face value, the notion of the singular, integrated self/soul is the dominant way in which theology and psychology have thought about the human person. However, just below the surface, is a wealth of theological and psychological models as well as our own reflection on the multiplicity of thoughts, emotions, and social roles that contribute to an ever growing awareness of the multi-dimensionality of each person. The theological and psychological models that support healthy human psychological multiplicity will be key components in the forthcoming chapters; for now, it is helpful simply to consider the experiential dimension of multiplicity. Simply stated, human psychological multiplicity is evidenced when we notice the inner pull when "part of us wants to do A, and a different part of us wants to do B." We also utilize multiplicity when we notice our "inner kid" who would much rather play or rest than do "adulting" things. Finally, for now, multiplicity is in play even when we notice strong emotions like anger, shame, or sadness take over our emotional awareness but know that there is more to us—in the midst of anger, we retain our capacity for compassion; in the midst of depression, our ability to acknowledge gratitude is still possible.

For survivors of trauma, the natural multiplicity of the person is essential for fully honoring the felt sense of the traumatic injury *and* holding onto the great variety of resources a person has for resiliency. Traumatic experience and post traumatic processing can lead part of a person to feel utterly dismayed, broken, or shattered; however, those feelings and self perception aren't the whole story. Parts of us hold violation, shame, betrayal; other parts of us hold our capacity to function, continue to hope (even if only a bit), and persevere. And, there is something even more that holds all the parts of us together. For trauma survivors, the great variety in multiplicity is important. It is what allows one to remain grounded while also being present to the parts of oneself that are unstable to the point, at times, of even threatening one's life. It is also the multiplicity within the care giver that allows one to be present in the face of narratives of horror, care for the variety of emotions and accompanying body sensations that arise within, and remain a compassionate and courageous witness.

The fourth foundational commitment for the construction of a trauma-sensitive theology and religious praxis is robust faith in human resiliency. One of the most damaging mistakes theologians, clergy, pastoral care providers, mental health care professionals, and lay people make with regard to trauma survivors is to buy into and further the feeling of brokenness that survivors experience. It is understandable and common for survivors of traumatic experience/s, especially when in the heat of post-traumatic response and processing, to feel "broken," "shattered," or "ruined." There is a part of many survivors that bears the burden of the weight of traumatic experience and processing. Additionally, the path of processing trauma is often ugly, messy, and can threaten to undo life. However, these concerns, suspicions, fears, and/or emotions of being fundamentally broken are just one dimension of the experience of processing trauma. They matter and honoring the concerns and fears is important; however, it is not the whole, existential, ontological truth. Theologians and clergy who buy into this legitimate feeling as absolute truth fundamentally undermine the very sources and resources for recovery and resiliency. Trauma-sensitive theology and praxis holds resolutely and fiercely, prescriptively and descriptively to the capacity for and offering of trauma processing, recovery, and resiliency when a person and/or community is provided the support and guidance required for negotiating post-traumatic response and processing.

The path towards resiliency is often long and arduous. Many who survive trauma don't receive adequate support to thrive or even to survive post-traumatic response. The struggle, loss, pain, fear, and desperation to cope with the aftermath of trauma is a weight that does threaten to undo, break or shatter; however, the threat does not have to be the end.

All mammals,[1] human beings included, have a vast array of resources for processing trauma. Peter Levine, Pat Ogden, Babette Rothschild, Susan McConnell and Richard Schwartz, and Bessel van der Kolk[2] all point to the variety of ways in which our bodies react to trauma and then respond to process the trauma. Francine Shapiro's development of Eye Movement Desensitization and Reprocess (EMDR) is the go-to treatment for the cognitive dimension of traumatic memory processing. Numerous movement traditions, including trauma-sensitive yoga, Feldenkrais, Nia, and drum circles, combine body movements, spiritual traditions, and communal practices to facilitate the processing of trauma and support of community in cultivating resiliency. Resiliency, the capacity to "bounce back" (even when "back" is always different), is a tremendous gift. It emerges from that place within the human person that is protected during trauma by the sacrifices of other parts of us that incur the injury. It is fostered through compassionate, courageous curiosity and care for all the parts of us. It is the hope and promise that keeps us going through the dark process of trauma recovery. Faith in resiliency must be protected and nourished for grace and life to have the enduring word.

FOR THE COMPANIONS

The hope and intent of this book is to provide religious care professionals and laity with a robust enough awareness of traumatic experience, processing, and resiliency to equip them as supportive, compassionate, informed companions to those walking the path of post-traumatic response and processing. While there are several insightful texts already available to clergy that focus on relational psychoanalytic perspectives of trauma[3] or handbooks for establishing church responses to abuse,[4] there are few texts designed for clergy that discuss the predominant learnings of clinician-scholar-researchers who focus their vocation in the area of trauma and dissociation. The hope of this text is to offer another theoretical, clinical

---

1. See Bradshaw, *Elephants on the Edge*.

2. Levine, *Waking the Tiger*; Ogden, Minton, and Pain, *Trauma and the Body*; Rothschild, *The Body Remembers*; McConnell, "Embodying the Internal Family, in *Internal Family Systems Therapy*, 90–106; van der Kolk, *The Body Keeps the Score*.

3. Cooper-White, *Many Voices*; Cooper-White, *Braided Selves*; and Swain, *Trauma and Transformation*.

4. Coleman, *The Dinah Project*, and Marie Fortune, *Sexual Violence*.

perspective, in addition to those already utilizing psychoanalytic lenses, for understanding traumatic response and accompanying dissociative processes that are common in people diagnosed with traumatic stress disorders. That said, this book is not intended to serve as training to assume the role of primary care giver for someone who is processing trauma. Trauma psychotherapy is a specialized area of mental health care and should not be taken on unless the care provider is a licensed mental health professional with post-graduate training in trauma specific modalities. The presence of a trauma psychotherapist does not negate nor diminish the need for a cloud of supportive witnesses. By understanding the journey of traumatic experience/s, response, process, and resiliency, religious care professionals and laity are more likely to be a helpful traveler and less likely to misinterpret traumatic response and unintentionally re-traumatize or shame survivors.

The first half of the book provides lenses for understanding trauma; the second half is an offering of constructive, systematic theology. I firmly believe that theology matters! The theology we believe, preach, and enact informs and creates the world we live in. Theological systems that offer an unyielding, legalistic god generate societies that are rigid, absolute, and morally dogmatic. If our theological understanding of human beings is summarily that of a "rot gut sinner," then where is there hope for resiliency? When our theological hope is confined to a paradise at the end of time, where do we marshal the resources to care for the planet, other creatures, and one another? Theology does indeed matter and requires informed engagement with society and the world. So, a theology that is ignorant of trauma process is more likely to harm than to offer good news. However, a theology that is sensitive to the struggle of traumatic experience, process, and recovery is positioned to offer more grace and hope to persons and/or communities harmed by traumatic violence. The constructive theology section of the text is offered as simply one way to think through our theological commitments in the face of trauma. It is the beginning of the theological work that can hopefully inform preaching, liturgy, and care.

The secondary intended audience of this text is mental health professionals. Mental health has a relatively long history of disconnection from religious communities and the spiritual commitments and experiences that often form and inform the lives of our clients. Just as theology matters for religious communities, it also matters for individuals. The guiding pillars that shape our early understandings of the world are often informed by our religious communities, whether or not we grew up as a member of a religious community. The ways in which we make sense of our place in the world, our connections to others, and our relationship to a divine energy, whatever form that takes, is our personal theology—even when it is an a-theology (atheism). As most psychotherapists and clergy know, there is little that can shake the very foundations of our established faith as much as experiences of traumatic violence and/or loss. While some of the trauma specific material in the first part may be known to mental health providers, I also retain the hope that other sections may provide therapists with compassionate and thoughtful options for engaging clients in their struggle to reconstruct their faith.

SURVEY OF THE TERRAIN

Trauma-Sensitive Theology: Thinking Theologically in the Era of Trauma provides religious scholars and educators, pastors, pastoral care givers, and theologically inclined laity an overview of traumatic responses in individuals and communities and resources for offering compassionate, informed, and helpful responses to survivors of traumatic experiences. The twenty-first century is rife with trauma: the falling of the Twin Towers on 9/11, the ongoing wars in the Middle East, the destabilization of government and economic structures, displacement of refugee populations, the prevalence of mass murders, domestic violence and sexual assault, and global climate change with escalating extreme weather patterns. While traumatic experiences have existed from the moment sentient beings have been present to experience violence and ruptures of safety that threaten life, individuals and communities living in the present century are inundated with news and images of traumatic events unlike inhabitants of prior centuries through the omnipresence of news platforms. While some of us are fortunate to escape direct experiences of trauma, none of us escape the ways in which trauma finds us through our smartphones, our news outlets, or the ways in which traumatic response weaves through culture. Traumatic experiences and news are all around us. Consequently, we are now living in an era of trauma.

While the impact and influence of traumatic response expands, theological scholarship has not adequately kept pace with the predominant need of our era. *Trauma-Sensitive Theology: Thinking Theologically in the Era of Trauma* fills the gap between the needs of trauma survivors and the knowledge available to those offering all forms of pastoral and theological care. It offers readers resources to understand various forms of trauma, patterns of traumatic response and recovery, and hermeneutical frames for theological thinking, pastoral care, and preaching that reduce the likelihood of re-traumatizing individuals and communities.

Part one, *Seeing Trauma*, focuses on how to notice traumatic processes in our lives and in our texts. In order for individuals, community care givers and leaders, and society to respond with appropriate care to survivors of traumatic events, we must first be able to identify the variety of ways in which traumatic experiences and responses manifest in our lives, families, community, society, and culture.

Chapter 1, "Identifying Trauma," aims to provide a variety of lenses to identify trauma. Trauma is generally only recognized when it is the consequence of prescribed crisis events in the life of an individual. While experiences like combat, assault, or natural disasters have a high correlation with post traumatic responses, trauma is not limited to these categories. This chapter discusses trauma as a response rather than an event and provides a basic template for recognizing the phases of traumatic processing. It discusses the challenges of acknowledging trauma, the dynamics of traumatic wounding, response, processing, and resiliency and the variety of ways traumatic response is present in individuals, society, and culture. The primary argument of this chapter is that trauma is a wounding in need of care *not* an ontological category of brokenness or annihilation. When we can begin to gain awareness of the many ways in which traumatic response shows up in our lives, communities, and culture, we are more fully equipped to offer resources for care and resiliency.

Chapter 2 discusses the impact and features of post traumatic response. It begins with a survey of the Internal Family Systems (IFS) model of psychotherapy as a lens for acknowledging, understanding, and caring for traumatic responses. IFS posits natural, adaptive, and functional human psychological multiplicity in which all parts of self are welcome and valued. While all parts may not be functioning with the most currently adaptive relational strategies, they all hold beneficial intentions and resources for authentic living once unburdened from past wounds. IFS also posits the presence of Self as the point of connection between the divine and human individual. Self is present in every being and remains even throughout horrific trauma and wounding. The "Impact of Trauma" extends through multiple dimensions of being and life including our biological systems, somatic perceptions, psychological and cognitive processes, relational attachments, and connection to the divine.

Chapter 3 focuses on "Cultivating Practices of Resiliency after Trauma." Fostering resiliency within communities and individuals who have experienced traumatic wounding often requires external support from compassionate and informed care providers. This chapter discusses the role of clergy and other religious and spiritual care givers as adjunct support to mental health care and primary care givers in the cultivation of healthy community attachments and ritual processes. It explores the key features of clinical care for trauma process and invites imaginative curiosity into how these features are already present in or could easily be incorporated into the ritual and healing practices of spiritual communities. Religious and spiritual communities have been the home of rituals and practices of healing for centuries all across the globe. The wisdoms infused within our traditions and ritual practices remain present, even when our attention to particular dimensions (somatic wisdom, sensory connections, and communal rhythms) have diminished in favor of increased cognitive engagement. Reclamation of these strands within our traditions only requires a shift in attention, intention, and purposeful connection.

Chapter 4 explores how we communicate about trauma within religious communities. The choice to perpetuate silence about experiences and consequences of traumatic wounding is no longer an option for responsible caretaking of souls and communities. The prevalence of trauma across forms and intensities requires compassionate and wise religious and spiritual leaders to acknowledge the presence of trauma in our sacred texts, interpretative choices, community leadership, and social engagement. This chapter offers several lenses for interpreting and communicating the presence of traumatic wounding in our lives, communities, and larger society. Specifically, it begins to explore the social privilege of non-primary traumatization as a framework for generating increased awareness of the social toll of living with traumatic response. Failing to acknowledge one's position in relation to traumatization risks generating blind spots within our personal experience that have the potential of further wounding survivors of trauma. The second subsection offers four hermeneutical lenses for the cultivation of trauma-sensitive theology and praxis: the hermeneutics of alterity, multiplicity, empathy, and accountability. These lenses can function bi-directionally in illuminating the presence and impact of trauma narratives within our sacred texts and as a path for honoring narratives of trauma in our lives and communities. The third subsection honors our sacred texts as tremendous resources for persons, communities, and societies coping with traumatic experience and response. They offer points of empathic resonance to hold our initial affective and behavioral responses to wounding thereby allowing us space to process and cultivate resiliency.

Part two of this volume offers a relatively brief systematic, constructive trauma-sensitive theology. The intention of this part of the text is to demonstrate one way of theological inquiry and construction that takes seriously the prevalence, consequence, and journey of recovery of traumatic exposure and wounding. It represents my focused theological journey over nearly twenty years as a systematic theologian, therapist, and minister in caring for those injured by trauma. While I am certain and hopeful that my thinking and articulation of the Christian faith will continue to develop and be refined by my own continued journey as a healing professional, this current form is a reflection of my desire to offer an internally consistent, trauma informed, theological confession that resonates with the impulse for trauma recovery and resiliency. I anticipate that readers who are strongly wed to specific theological traditions codified prior to the twentieth century may experience some resistance in my articulation of faith. Tension that arises in response to a new way of thinking when it challenges our previously held structures and categories of understanding is natural and normative. For those readers who have felt constrained or unmet by other theological systems or who struggle to integrate contemporary knowledge with theological systems from a previous era of knowing, I hope that the avenues present in this part of the text can open up avenues for renewed engagement with the divine and communities of faith.

With humility, I join with and echo Paul Tillich's sentiment: "Whether or not I am able to agree with [valuable criticism or conversation of the substance of my thought] I gladly accept it as a valuable contribution to the continuous theological discussion between theologians and within each theologian. But I cannot accept criticism as valuable which merely insinuates that I have surrendered the substance of the Christian message because I have used a terminology which consciously deviates from the biblical or ecclesiastical language. Without such deviation, I would not have deemed it worthwhile to develop a theological system for our period."[5] The intensity and presence of traumatic stimuli in our time requires us to examine with fresh eyes many of the theological constructs, including our understanding

5. Tillich, *Systematic Theology*, vol. 2, viii.

of God (Theology proper) and divine presence, that resonated strongly in other eras but now have more potential to wound than offer care.

Part two is composed of a four part journey that seeks to place experiences of "before" trauma, the wounding of trauma, and the desire for reconnection and attunement in parallel with traditional systematic loci. On one hand, the designations of chapter breaks are fairly arbitrary. Systematic theology, when done well, should naturally flow from one loci of focus to another with each point reflecting what has already been covered and illuminating the areas to come. On the other hand, they reflect a natural progression in our theological categories that reflect the journey of traumatic wounding and recovery. The four primary commitments that inform trauma-sensitive theology (primacy of bodily experience, full acceptance of trauma narratives, natural given-ness of human psychological multiplicity, and faith in the robust resiliency of trauma survivors) are the foundation of this constructive work. Though they are not always brought into the foreground, they do always reside under, with, and through this theological work.

Chapter 5, "Pre-Traumatic Creation," houses the theological prolegomena, exploration of ontology, quality of divine power, and doctrine of creation. Drawing on the open, process, and relational theology work of Catherine Keller and others, this chapter imagines a place for the energy and matter of the "before" as good and generative of the structures of our world and being. Chapter 6, "Traumatic Disruption," explores humanity as the imago of a Trinitarian relational divinity, defines sin as abuses of relational power, and identifies Jesus as the one who never abused his relational power but was traumatized by abuses of institutional power unto death. The twofold identification of Jesus as sinless and as victim of traumatizing wounds highlights the presence of trauma at the very heart of Christian identity and community. If the central event of Christianity is an experience of traumatizing death, how can we not take seriously the impact of trauma and the path of resiliency?

Chapter 7, "Restoring Connection," discusses the eclipsing of divine connection as a consequence of sin and looks to theological options of soteriology to pave a way towards renewing connections internally, relationally, ecologically, and with God. What models of atonement offer visions of restored relationality that resonate with our understanding of sin as abuses of relational power? Do the traditional options of atonement present a means of atonement that fosters recovery or contribute to established systems of power that are more apt towards harm than healing? Chapter 8 "Enhancing Attunement" focuses on the theological loci of pneumatology, ecclesiology, and ethics as a path towards honoring the presence of divine energy in the world and in communities. The Spirit of the fullness of life seeks to infuse all living organisms and entities within creation with connection to divine energy that sustains us all. When we are better able to care for the wounds that block our access to divine energy, we are more capable of fulfilling our authentic presence and place in the world.

Finally, the conclusion invites cohesive reflection on the intersections of the two major parts of the text. Doing theology is a religious and relational practice with commitments to authentically speak to the presence of the Divine in the world as we encounter it. It also requires us to speak on behalf of a community. Trauma-sensitive theology is one attempt to engage both sets of commitments with an awareness to the prevalence of traumatic wounding in multiple dimensions of our personal and social lives. The reach of traumatic wounding is perhaps more engrossing than at other points in human history, due in part to the vast acceleration of media technology in the past century. As religious leaders and care giving professionals, how will we respond to this pervasive need? What shall we say to survivors of primary trauma or our congregations who live with an ever increasing level of underlying anxiety and uncertainty? How shall we offer care? The final section discusses the importance of Self care, boundaries as a form of care, the mandate to do no harm, and reflections on the quality of attuned care.

The primary intention of trauma-sensitive theology is to offer a way of thinking through the many loci of our theological systems that honors the experience of traumatic wounding and takes into account the journey of experiences of trauma, traumatic response, processing of trauma, and promoting resiliency. It emerged from decades of my own work as a theologian, pastor, therapist, and survivor in conjunction with my disappointment and then anger at how survivors of trauma are treated and talked about by those in the care giving professions. This manuscript is my offering towards the hope that survivors of trauma will be met with compassion for the struggle, knowledgeable empathy, appreciation of survival strategies, and a tenacious hope and faith in the human capacity for recovery and resiliency. Trauma does wound; it doesn't have to break.

PART ONE

Seeing Trauma

1

Identifying Trauma

The task of recognizing traumatic experience and post traumatic response is deceptively challenging. The challenge rises primarily from humanity's innate predisposition to turn away in disbelief from experiences that counter our desire for a safe enough world. Judith Herman, whose book *Trauma and Recovery*[1] is considered a classic text in trauma studies and a go-to introduction to trauma, notes the history of society's "episodic amnesia" of trauma itself. The study of trauma is chock full of fits and starts: from Freud's early work with Bauer that acknowledged connections between experiences of incest and subsequent psychological difficulties,[2] to the waves of attention and neglect offered to veterans of war. It seems as if even the study of trauma itself is historically threatening. The naming of experience/s and associated responses as trauma first requires a prolonged tolerance of acknowledging that human beings are capable of violating societal norms and cultural taboos at a far greater incidence than is comfortable and secondly demands some kind of response from those who are awakened to traumatic violations and violence.

Theologically, we have traditionally named experiences that correlate with trauma as "evil." While the theological concept of evil is helpful in at least naming those experiences and behaviors that threaten the stability and sustainability of life and relationship, it can also be troublesome when it is preached as a sharp binary with the "good" or holy. The black and

1. Herman, *Trauma and Recovery*.

2. Freud and Bauers, *Study of Hysterics*. Following professional criticism of their correlation of incest and psychological suffering, Freud shifted the focus of his work from experiences of trauma to the variety of drives and desires in a person.

white, rigid thinking that underlays the good/evil binary can unwittingly limit theological and pastoral responses to traumatized survivors of violence. This binary is particularly detrimental in instances of chronic child abuse when the child already depends on the perpetrator of violence for survival, when behaviors are conflated with identity, or when the behavior of perpetrators is taken in and internalized as shame by the survivor.

Socially, our attention to traumatic experience and response has historically fallen into an all or nothing binary. In moments of social crisis, our social attention and imagination are beckoned to attention to traumatic wounding and response. When we are able, attention to and funding for research and programs to facilitate recovery from traumatic response dissipates and our cultural imagination "forgets." On the flip side, when attention to traumatic experience/s becomes a topic and norm of popular culture there can be a minimization of the consequences and struggle of trauma recovery. When everything is "abusive," then experiences of traumatizing abuse are rendered invisible in the cacophony of popular uses of the language. For example, I was at a pastoral care conference several years ago when an established scholar in the community described his experience of being charged $2.50 for a bottle of water as being "raped." When we use language of violence and assault to describe our displeasure at normal life events, we are robbing survivors of violence and assault of the very language that holds the depth and gravity of their experiences.

How we use language in discussing traumatizing experience and post traumatic response is important. The language we use to describe our experiences can exaggerate, minimize, or accurately reflect the significance and impact of what occurs. How we choose to speak about and understand what occurs is influenced by what our society can or will tolerate. Mary Daly offers four strategies people and society employ to deny systems that perpetuate harm including the sexual caste system and institutional oppression. The four options described by Daly are 1) trivialization (i.e., experiences of harm are minimized in comparison—"sexual assault is important, but no more so than poverty, war, or climate change"); 2) particularization (i.e., one manifestation of harm is valued as more significant thereby limiting the claim of those who experience different forms—"his trauma is 'worse' than mine"); 3) spiritualization (i.e., traumatic suffering is classified as a burden to bear akin to Jesus's suffering on the cross—"this experience is God's way of testing your faith"); and 4) universalization (i.e., "all people suffer and encounter experiences that are bad and who is to say that your experience is worse than others?").[3] These four strategies highlighted by Daly are regularly employed in response to disclosures of traumatizing experience. They infiltrate our social understandings of traumatic experience, our personal struggles with traumatic responses, and our offerings of hope and resiliency from trauma. When those who offer support underestimate the prevalence of sexual assault, child abuse, or war trauma, we are more likely to retraumatize the survivors in our midst by unintentionally trivializing the experience or response to trauma, misnaming psychological processing as a sign of a lack of faith, minimizing the struggle of post traumatic response or foreclosing on resources of resiliency, or expanding the category of trauma to include experiences and responses that pose a challenge to life but do not meet the criteria of traumatic overwhelm or response.

KNOWING OURSELVES

When clinicians, scholars, clergy, or others in the helping professions refer to survivors of traumatic experience/s, there is a temptation to see the person solely in the terms of their experience with trauma. This phenomenon is present, and criticized, with regard to mental or physical health medical diagnosis. People become the "cutter," the "borderline," "stage three cancer," or the "hip replacement." In other areas of life, we become defined by our professions, our hobbies, or our relationships. The labels that we attribute to ourselves or to others have a social function that can be helpful; yet, they can never capture the fullness of who a person is and how they live in the world. The degree to which a particular label or social designation sticks and encompasses personal or social identity largely depends on how integral that label is to our self-understanding. If I decide that the most significant dimension of who I am as a person is my sexual orientation and it becomes one of the core, centralizing features of my self, then my social identity label as gay, bi, trans, or straight will direct how I engage in the world. If I decide, or learn via social conditioning, that is it of utmost important to be "pretty" and meet the criteria of beauty, then I will make decisions that will amplify my ability to be successful in performing beauty. If we teach boys that "real men" are tough, stoic, rich, and use power (even violence) to obtain desires, then we place traits of a particular form of masculinity (which is often toxic to the individual, family, and society) in a more central identity category.

3. Daly, *Beyond God the Father*, 5.

Likewise, when we view personal experiences or others' experiences with traumatic response and traumatizing events as central to identity, it can become the default way in which survivors of trauma live in the world and how care providers see those to whom we provide care. All of us have a great variety of personal identity markers that collectively make us who we are; health and wisdom come when all the dimensions that make us who we are are welcome in our awareness and work in harmony with one another.

WHAT TRAUMA IS AND WHAT IT IS NOT

One of the highly seductive beliefs that individuals and communities have is to equate one part of us with the whole of who we are. This tendency is especially seductive when one part of us requires or claims a large amount of space within the person. Parts that tend to claim a lot of space are those that are either significantly wounded, burdened, or those that keep us distracted from our experiences of wounding. The word "trauma" etymologically derives from the Greek word meaning "wound." Trauma at its most fundamental level means wounding. Wounding can occur when a part of who we are is exiled by societal structures (sexual orientation or institutional racism), family norms (expectations of achievement, appearance, or performance), personal expectations (feelings of being "not good/smart/pretty/etc. enough), or life experiences that fundamentally challenge our belief of who we are or how the world works. The more integral the wounded and exiled part of us is to our self-understanding, the greater the felt impact will be and the more other parts of the person will respond in increasingly rigid and demonstrative ways.

Wounding, whether it is physical, psychological, relational, or spiritual, can occur in a variety of settings throughout life—from our earliest years when our cries for comfort and physical needs are met with either neglect or overbearing expectations, to our development as we negotiate the losses of divorce, death, or violence. These injuries can be traumatizing wounds or can remain non-traumatizing wounds that heal via the innate biological and psychological systems of normal processing and repair. Traumatic wounding often occurs when we experience a crisis event or violence. Crisis events include natural disasters, assault, death of a loved one, loss of vocation, home, or ability, and an array of other experiences (including those listed in the diagnostic criteria for traumatic stress disorders in the DSM-5) or a significant threat to life. Crisis events often precipitate responses designated as (big-t) Trauma. Socially, we understand and have compassion for the presence of traumatic wounding and response after experiencing crisis events. It makes sense to us collectively that participating in war, experiencing sexual assault, or losing your home to fire or hurricane flooding would generate feelings of overwhelm, anxiety, terror, despair, etc.

The connection between crisis events and how human beings respond to those events sometimes leads us to draw such a tight connection that we being to think the events themselves are trauma. We begin to presume that the crisis event, and by extraction only crisis events, leads to trauma. It is important to key into the possibility of traumatic response in the wake of crisis events; however, it is a mistake to limit our awareness of trauma responses solely to crisis events. The risk in the mistake is that we become more vulnerable to missing out on other prevalent, significant contexts that also traumatize people and communities. Many times it is the "quiet," unseen, chronic conditions of systemic and/or relational abuse and violation that generate the most entrenched patterns of traumatic response. These ongoing experiences become habituated and consequently are bypassed in our thinking about crisis. More tragically, it is these recurring, ongoing, or chronic violations that escape awareness, evade our efforts of care, and are distanced from our collective attention. We take on the very amnesia or denial that recurrently plagues our attempts to care for those wounded by crisis and violation.

Whether the precipitating experience is a crisis event or chronic violation or neglect, "trauma" is the response to an experience/s not the event experienced. Exposure to crisis events and chronic violation or neglect set the stage for the development of traumatic wounding; however, there is not a 1:1 correlation. The additional factor that significantly influences whether or not an experience will generate a traumatic wound is the combination of the vulnerability of the person or community prior to the event/s and the degree of support, empathy, and resources present before and after the event to facilitate processing of the experience. A person's vulnerability to traumatic wounding includes environmental, social, demographic, and biological risk factors that encompass socioeconomic level, history of prior mental health distress, level of education, heart rate variability, and dynamics within family of origin.[4] Becoming aware of the vulnerability of developing a traumatic response simply means acknowledging that each person emerges from their own particular social, relational environment with varying resources of support.

4. Halligan and Yehuda, "Risk Factors for PTSD."

We all have a unique set of experiences of receiving support and lacking support that form our internal psychological world. This is a statement of occurrence far more than of judgment or valuation. Each individual takes within themselves experiences of care, neglect, support, friendship, discord, judgment, accomplishment, falling short, hope, and expectations. These unique clusterings of experiences build the resources for our resiliency just as they also generate vulnerabilities. If I don't have enough support to succeed, part of me learns that the world is a place of scarcity and disappointment while another part of me learns the importance of tenacity. If I have more than enough financial and relational resources to easily meet my goal, part of me learns that there is more than enough in the world while another part of me learns that meeting goals should be easy for me and I may fail to cultivate the skills needed to persevere in the face of obstacles. In both cases, vulnerabilities emerge alongside capacities for resiliency—the trick is finding and supporting a healthy balance.

The other key component in whether or not crisis events or chronic harm will result in traumatic wounding is the presence and type of social response. From the time we are little and throughout our lives, our first response to hurt is to reach out for support and compassion. The toddler falls, scrapes her knee, and cries out for mom. If mom is attentive enough, she will witness the scrape on the child's knee, acknowledge the injury, provide care either through kisses or band-aids as appropriate, and then send the toddler back into her activity. This innate movement of care that includes witnessing, mirroring, care taking of the wound, and reassurance sets the template for how we give and receive care when we are wounded. If the mother is not attentive and caring enough to complete the ritual of care and misses one or more components, the child will learn over time that she cannot count on others to meet her in her distress; while her physical wound may heal, the emotional/relational wound remains and develops into a burden that part of her carries into future life and relationships. The importance of appropriate social support following crisis events extends beyond the individual into how communities heal or struggle with resiliency in the aftermath of disaster. Consider the impact of the absence of support and care in the aftermath of Hurricane Katrina. For many survivors, the loss of home was significantly wounding and compounded by the feelings of hopelessness and despair that came from the experience of remaining on roofs for days and other forms of lack of rescue. The experience of being alone in the midst of crisis is often more trauma-inducing than the crisis alone.

When a person's vulnerabilities exceed their internal and external resources of support and stabilization, traumatic wounding occurs. Traumatic wounding is the overwhelming of a person's somatic and psychological systems. These systems are part of the focus in the next chapter. All mammals have wonderful somatic/body processes for dispelling overwhelm from our bodies. In the animal realm, this process is most easily seen in the shaking movements of prey animals who have escaped capture. It is the way in which their bodies expel residual hormones and neurochemicals that allowed animals to succeed in their fight/flight response with minimal overwhelm. Psychologically, we all have mechanisms for processing emotional material that facilitates its movement from immediate experience to short term memory and finally into long term memory. When our body processes are unable to escape to safety either physically or psychologically, we freeze or shut down. The process of freezing dampens sensation so that we are buffered from experiencing the full pain of the impending injury. While this biological strategy is advantageous in the midst of crisis, it also is more likely to result in traumatic overwhelm and response. The experience of somatic and psychological overwhelm accompanied by an absence of "good enough" social support interrupts the innate systems of recovery and is traumatic wounding.

It is vital to clearly state and understand that traumatic wounding is an *injury*; it is NOT ontology. Survivors of traumatizing experience/s and processing are not fundamentally "shattered,"[5] "annihilated souls,"[6] or individuals "whose lives had been so dramatically undone by violence, that try as they may, they could not seem to get the existential foothold on life that they needed to become active church participants and productive theology students, to say nothing of becoming generally happy people."[7] These descriptions of individuals who have survived trauma, offered by theological leaders working in the area of religion and trauma, are inherently pathologizing and woefully neglect the inherent resiliency of human beings. To be clear, traumatic wounding when not supported, processed, and cared for can undermine a person's stability, daily function, and even survival; however, traumatic wounding is not a final word. It is an injury that, like most other injuries to the body, is not automatically or necessarily terminal or debilitating (though some are). Holding both the weight of the wound,

5. Rambo, *Spirit and Trauma*.

6. Shooter, *How Survivors of Abuse Relate to God*.

7. Jones, *Trauma and Grace*.

the burden of traumatic processing and recovery, and the hope and potential for resiliency (or even flourishing) in appropriate tension is a dynamic challenge—and a requirement for those of us who seek to provide support through the journey.

DEFINING TERMS/TRACING PROCESS

Within the psychotherapy and traumatology professional community there are a variety of potential paths available for framing and understanding traumatic exposure and recovery. Most begin with the establishment of safety, continue on to processing traumatic response, and conclude with incorporation of the traumatic experience into the long term narrative memory of the survivor. The techniques utilized for the middle portion of this trajectory vary according to the school of thought that influences the clinician or model. Practitioners who emerge from one of the traditions with roots in psychoanalysis may employ techniques like hypnosis. Those who think of what ails us as disruptions in family systems and attachment utilize techniques that facilitate the formation of more secure attachments. Clinicians schooled in behavioral or cognitive psychology highlight the ways in which traumatic experiences disrupt healthful thinking work with the protocols of trauma-focused cognitive behavioral therapy. Pastoral counselors who maintain a keen eye on the role of faith and moral character illuminate the ways in which injury occurs when our behavior violates our moral standing and generate "moral injury."[8] Like many of life's most challenging dimensions, recovery from traumatic wounding is best supported when it attends to all dimensions of human self awareness and being—cognitive, spiritual, relational, emotional, and somatic.

Returning to Judith Herman for a moment, Herman identifies the five "stages of recovery" as "a healing relationship, safety, remembrance and mourning, reconnection, and commonality," as outlined in part two of her classic text.[9] These stages are quite helpful for clinicians who are encountering survivors who are already at the point of seeking assistance. For those helping professionals, like clergy, it is facilitative to broaden the frame. People in community and congregations may be in the midst of traumatic response (initial or post-) for an extended period of time before they are at a place to seek guidance in processing. With that in mind, what are the

8. Brock and Lettini, *Soul Repair.*

9. Herman, *Trauma and Recovery*, 133–235.

components of the full arc of trauma including some of the indicators of pre-therapeutic trauma presentation?

In the immediate aftermath of a crisis event, whether a single episode or an additional episode in chronic trauma, a person's survival system kicks into gear. Some people, in the face of crisis, run towards danger with the hopes of assisting others, run away from danger in order to survive, or freeze in place and are psychologically and/or physically unable to react. The next chapter will cover some of the reasons why there is a significant variety of responses. For now, it is important to note the variety and make the claim that all types of survival mechanisms are good if they result in survival. There is no "right" or "wrong" way to survive crisis events and the option a person employs emerges from a variety of factors including family of origin, likelihood of survival, attachments to others also in danger, etc. Once the crisis event/episodes conclude, survivors enter into a period of post-traumatic response.

Post-traumatic response can be short lived or continue for decades. Indicators of post-traumatic response are those delineated in the criteria for traumatic stress disorders in the DSM and include symptoms that can present on either the "too much" or "too little" ends of a myriad of scales including, but not limited to, arousal, vigilance, and control. The hallmark of post-traumatic response is the challenge of regulating body, mind, emotions, and relationships to sustain a flexible, responsive balance to normative life events. Too often, people connect post-traumatic response with the less pro-social end of the scale. We easily identify the person struggling with post-traumatic responses that include social dysfunctions: difficulty maintaining employment, engaging in destructive relationships, drinking, drug use, eating disorders, etc. However, on the other end of the scale are many pro-social manifestations of "too much/too little" post-traumatic response including perfectionism, people pleasing, exaggerated work ethic, over emphasis on exercise, etc. Manifestations of post-traumatic response that are in alignment with and get reinforced by social norms are more often overlooked, especially in cases when a person is a survivor of chronic traumatization in childhood and early adolescence. The phase of post-traumatic response potentially includes a risk to continued life either via suicide or ongoing practices of self-medication that harm vital organs.

The duration and intensity of post-traumatic response is highly variable and extends into the phase of traumatic processing. The task of processing traumatic injury/ies garners the most clinical attention and is the phase in which persons intentionally work to free up the neurological, psychological, somatic, and relational dynamics that got stalled or stuck in the experience/s of traumatic exposure. Traumatic processing can be risky, stressful, terrifying, and/or debilitating, especially if strategies for maintaining safety and the rate of processing is not sufficiently managed and cared for; yet, it is a necessity for authentic resiliency and recovery. There is no way around—only through. Processing the components of traumatic experiences requires re/collecting the dimensions of the experience that got disconnected and stuck when the person's system was overwhelmed. It is a re-combining of the thoughts, internal and external sensations, behaviors, and emotions into a coherent and cohesive whole that can be processed and joined with other experiences that were not wounding so that the person is no longer held captive to the reactionary pulls of post traumatic response.

Resiliency is basically finding your feet and beginning again with balance and authenticity. A tragic reality of traumatic experience is that there is no going back. The person you were prior to trauma has changed. This change does not have to be all doom and gloom. It's not the end of *the* world; but it is the end of *a* world. The beliefs that correspond to living in the world prior to experiences of trauma are transformed and the loss of the "before" gets to be grieved and mourned. Consequently, resiliency isn't a "going back" or "living as if that/those bad things didn't happen." It's not "forgive and forget." Resiliency is the courage to face the darkness of traumatic injury, process and care for the wounds, and come to new ways of living authentically. Let me be very clear; traumatic wounding is never a divine pedagogical tool or redeemable as a "good." When survivors of trauma take their experiences and wrest from those wounds profound empathy for others, wisdom in both the hopes and depths of loss and sorrow, or robust strength, it is done *in spite* of traumatic wounding that truly threatened life. Resiliency from trauma is not a guarantee and, tragically, many people and communities don't make it to recovery. When resiliency is accessed and supported, it is testament to the combination of the painfully difficult work of processing trauma, the presence of "enough" social support to sustain survival, and the good fortune to have access to resources (internal, external, and financial) that facilitate recovery. The journey of recovery and resiliency is an ongoing path for most survivors that continues throughout life. It is rarely a "now completed, obtained, and moving on free and clear" experience.

The symptoms, challenges, and features of post traumatic response and traumatic processing present along a spectrum of intensity. It is not a question of present/not present; but an assessment of *how* present. Symptoms of post traumatic response, including hypervigilance, self-medicating (with a great variety of means to regulate anxiety or dissociation), insomnia, and flashbacks can be present as minimally disruptive to daily living or can dominate how a person lives their life. When symptoms of traumatic response and post traumatic response are at a high enough intensity to interfere with a person's ability to function, they are designated as a "clinical presentation." This simply means that there is enough disruption that additional and/or professional support is needed to facilitate processing to return to a functional way of living. In other words, symptoms are getting in the way of life too much. When the intensity of post traumatic responses are too much, they also generally meet the diagnostic criteria for ASD or PTSD in the DSM.

Not all post traumatic responses reach the intensity designated by "clinical presentation"; some people and communities experience challenges to authentic and full living related to post traumatic response that are "subclinical." Subclinical simply indicates that symptoms of post traumatic response are present but the individual is still able to hold things together well enough. Now, "well enough" frequently still falls short of a person's hopes and vision of crafting and living into an authentic life. It is to some degree functional but still a challenge or struggle. Subclinical presentations of post traumatic response also require processing and the journey of processing trauma almost always requires some form of support. Unfortunately, because people and communities with subclinical intensities of post traumatic response symptoms remain functional enough, they too often don't seek out or receive adequate care and support. Subclinical presentations of post traumatic response are still trauma responses. One of the challenges for clinicians, physicians, clergy, and other care professionals is how to destigmatize experiences of post traumatic response and how to design means of facilitating trauma processing and resiliency for those whose symptoms are unacknowledged and unnamed as trauma.

TYPES OF TRAUMA

Assessing and categorizing "types" of trauma is a peculiar task and like most ventures of demarcation is open to criticism from those who would make different choices related to grouping and identification. I will be upfront in confessing that there are many options for establishing categories of trauma. This section is intended to simply offer one way or lens for seeing trauma in the lives of our communities, families, or within ourselves. The grouping moves from clear, concrete, personal, and, readily acknowledged types of trauma to those that are more elusive, diffuse, and tend to impact greater numbers of people with less intensity. These more pervasive and broader types of trauma are often invisible yet continue to impact the ways in which persons negotiate society and cultivate relationships. Acknowledging the ways in which larger swaths of the population are impacted by broad trauma is not meant to indicate that the personal toll of broader forms of societal or cultural trauma are necessarily equal to primary trauma in the intensity of symptoms that challenge everyday life. There are important differences that require different strategies of processing and care. Until we can attend to the multivariate dimensions of the impact of trauma in our individual and collective lives, we are more prone to perpetuate behaviors, systems, and laws that continue to inflict primary traumatization.

Primary Traumatization

When most of us think about individuals struggling with traumatic processing, we tend to think of the war survivor with PTSD who flinches at the sound of gun fire or the survivor of sexual assault who struggles with continued daily functions in the immediate aftermath of violation. Both of these scenarios are examples of primary traumatization. People who develop a trauma response to a direct personal experience/s fall into the category of primary traumatization and frequently develop symptoms of post traumatic response that meet the intensity of clinical presentation. Primary traumatization can occur due to crisis events like natural disasters, assault, car accidents, and war. Additionally, primary traumatization can develop following surgery, heart attacks, financial ruin, or chronic abuse.

Secondary Traumatization

Secondary traumatization includes individuals or communities whose loved one is primarily traumatized. Secondary trauma can occur when a loved one's life is extinguished or threatened. This form of trauma is present in family members of those who complete suicide, parents and siblings of children with chronic or terminal illness, or caring professionals whose client population includes people with primary traumatization. In the professional realm, secondary trauma is also known as compassion fatigue and is a prime cause of burnout.[10] One of the primary emotional indicators of secondary trauma is the feeling of helplessness or hopelessness in attending to the harm of a loved one. Secondary trauma can reach the intensity of clinical presentation and activate many of the same symptoms present in primary trauma. Symptoms or indicators of secondary trauma can also remain at a subclinical threshold. In both cases, people struggling with secondary trauma can significantly benefit from engaging in the work of processing secondary trauma and movement towards resiliency.

Intergenerational Trauma

In popular culture and life, many people have an awareness of verses in the Bible that talk about the "sins of the father" being passed down to the "third and fourth generations" (Exod 20:5, 34:6–7). While there is fruitful conversation and textual analysis to be had on how to interpret these verses, I will leave the bulk of that conversation to scholars far more equipped than I in biblical studies and interpretation of ancient texts and cultures. For the purpose of this conversation, I mention these texts as a beginning for reflection on the ways in which experience/s of violence, either as victim or perpetrator, impact the family structure. When survivors of crisis events or ongoing relational violence or neglect are unwilling or unable to access resources for processing post traumatic responses and memories, it is common for those responses to turn into patterns of behavior that are unhealthy that are then modeled as normative. For instance, if we grow up in a household that is unstable due to domestic ab/use and child abuse or neglect, it is understandable that as adults we would either model the harmful behavior of our parent/s or organize our lives around being/behaving differently. This can show up as either adopting rigid rules and boundaries that keep emotional outbursts exiled or in the reenactments of harmful behavior and attachments. In cases of violence or addictive behaviors, intergenerational trauma can also leave a wave of primary trauma in its wake.

Intergenerational trauma generally presents subclinically as a maladaptive set of relational responses or beliefs about self and/or the world. For some, the wounds of intergenerational trauma get passed down through

10. van Dernoot Lipsky and Burk, *Trauma Stewardship.*

33

the explicit or implicit norms of the family. The norms of a family are the unwritten rules that everyone somehow instinctively knows about (e.g., "it is essential to achieve," "we don't talk about that," "everyone in our family goes to jail eventually," "our people drink a lot," "our people never drink," "no one is ever safe enough," etc.). Intergenerational trauma can also get passed down through modeling of familiar behavior, family norms, or through the combination of nature and nurture studied by the field of epigenetics. Epigenetics is the study of how our environment can alter which genes are expressed (or turned on) and which become inactive. The field of study is especially intriguing for future research and understanding of the impact of ongoing traumatic stress on an individual and family. What are the changes to the genome structure and expression when a person's nervous system is chronically dysregulated and forms a baseline of emotional and body regulation that is either wrung too tight due to hyper-arousal or too loose due to hypo-arousal? At the moment, these are still open questions but they might provide a helpful imperative for more resources to become available to traumatized persons and communities in upcoming decades.

Repeating the harms or "sins" of parents whose lives are marked by unprocessed post traumatic responses is not set in stone. Just because one receives the beliefs that emerge as initially protective towards future harm but are no longer needed or appropriate to current life does not mean that they need to remain a driving factor after becoming aware of how those beliefs are no longer adaptive.

Societal Trauma

Societal trauma is often prompted by a crisis event that is experienced, either in person or via prolonged media coverage, on a mass scale. The most stark occurrence in the current century for those residing in the United States is the terror attack on September 11, 2001. Other examples include the attack on Pearl Harbor, the explosion of the Challenger, the assassination of President Kennedy, and a vast array (far too many to list here) of mass shootings, war zones, and international terrorist attacks. Crisis events like these can induce trauma responses throughout the society. Most of us can describe where we were, how we felt, and who we were with when we first heard about or saw the images of the Challenger space shuttle explosion. I recall sitting on the floor in Ms. Arnett's third grade classroom and watching the launch on a TV sitting atop the very tall (for an 8 year old) rolling TV stand. On Tuesday, September 11, 2001, I stopped by the campus store after biology lecture to get something for breakfast when I caught glimpse of the TV and noticed that something weird was going on. A few minutes later the second tower was hit by the airplane. The rest of that day vacillates between clear recollections of walking back to campus to attend a college-wide service of information and mourning and complete lack of memory. Persons of prior generations can describe with clarity where they were when Kennedy was shot or when they learned of the attacks on Pearl Harbor. These national crisis events reverberate throughout society.

National crisis events have long impacted the citizens of the societies that were harmed during the crisis. However, in the late twentieth and early twenty-first century the proliferation of media technology has had a profound impact on the intensity of exposure to crisis events and the rate in which we become aware of individual crisis events and the primary traumatization of others. Smart phones have the capacity to bring information and videos of trauma into our pockets. Within minutes, we have data information about mass shootings in areas hundreds of miles away as well as video and social media posts of others expressing loss, panic, and fear. Videos from police car and vest cams depicting the murder of unarmed, often completely innocent, citizens are distributed via social media outlets. Increasingly through mediums like Facebook Live, incidents of murder are broadcast live and show up unexpectedly in our newsfeeds. The rabid increase of the availability and intensity of images and details of crisis events is a novel feature of contemporary society and is more likely to increase in intensity than abate in upcoming decades.

Increased visibility of crisis events and the primary traumatization of our fellow citizens generate the sense of being more present to the traumatic incident and more helpless in our capacity to physically assist in the care of others. This combination of feeling more present and less powerful in the immediacy increases the likelihood of post trauma responses in individuals viewing the crisis event as secondary traumatization. Post traumatic responses that are present in individuals can also present in the society's response to national crisis events. As a society, we can react with either too much or too little responses. On one hand, we rush the process of declaring war with due diligence of responsibility in an effort to assert power and vindicate our losses. On the other hand, we fail to respond appropriately in establishing effective safeguards against future crises like mass shootings or devastating flooding.

The tendency in societal manifestations of post traumatic response is to deepen a sense of tribalism by more clearly designating who gets to count as the "us" and who is designated as the "thems" who threaten our way of life. As time progresses with unprocessed societal post traumatic response, the divisions that initially were drawn in an effort to regain safety become entrenched and eventually tear apart the very fabric of society. It is a pattern visible in Germany following the sanctions imposed by the Treaty of Versailles and in the current rash and rise of xenophobia and intrasociety violence in the United States and Europe as entire swaths of the population are designated a threat to either safety or economic vitality. Communities already pushed to the margins of society are most vulnerable to intrasociety violence either as a reaction to perceived threats or as a means of denying the society's history of imposing violence as the perpetrators of the same types of harm they have now received from others. Violence directed towards those within exiled communities within the larger society is often a continuation of a lineage of genocide, in the case of Native American Nations, and slavery, in the case of African Americans. The deep and brutal violence inflicted on these populations within the United State continues in the exiling of Native Americans and disregard for their sovereign borders and the ghettoizing of African American communities that are regularly neglected by those who are responsible for the distribution of societal resources.

More subtly, the wounds inflicted throughout life by systemic abuses of power, such as systemic racism, misogyny, and homophobia and transphobia, which is present in a great variety and intensity of dimensions, propagate messages about who one is and what one's potential is that diminishes resources for authentic and fulfilling life. One of the more insidious dimensions of the exiling of marginalized communities and those who do not historically hold positions of societal power is the cancerous dynamic through which societal post traumatic response as a reaction to national crisis events or society's own history of perpetrating violence infects entire communities intergenerationally. The sins of the fathers do reverberate through society through the third, fourth, fifth generations.

Cultural Trauma

Cultural trauma is an outflow of societal trauma. When societal post traumatic response goes unprocessed for an extended period of time, it begins to find manifestation in the cultural products of a society. Like post traumatic response in individuals, when trauma remains in the body and soul, it will eventually find expression in cultural productions, dreams, and projects of creativity, like art, dance, film, music, literature, etc. Our bodies, individual, communal, and social, have natural and intuitive mechanisms for trying to process traumatic experiences and responses. Many of these mechanisms are body centered/somatic/biological or right-brain oriented mechanisms. In the years following a national crisis event, it is common to see a surge of movies with themes that reflect the event of trauma or the mood and emotions of the society post trauma. These cultural products are a gage of how well the society is processing their experiences. As marginalized communities emerge from societal exilation, their stories begin to be told in the larger social screen and often face a backlash from those parts of society who are not prepared to acknowledge their roles in perpetrating violence and harm.

When societal post traumatic response transmutes into cultural trauma, it has the potential to transform normative understandings of how the world works or our established metanarratives. Following World War II, atomic weaponry, and the Holocaust, the Enlightenment hopes of progress towards an eschatological utopia, the dependable stability of a central narrative of the world that worked for most people, and faith in rationality that guided the modern era came crashing down. In its ashes, emerged an understandable skepticism of the fundamental goodness of human rationality and the products of ingenuity and discovery that follow. Trust in the universality of cultural narratives refracted into a recognition of a multitude of narratives informed by an awareness of the importance of context. There is not one story of the colonization of the United States— the Eurocentric story that continues to be celebrated every November. The stories of the colonization of lands and births of nations is a multivariate story in which not all stories end happily ever after. The context of the story teller matters and as the well-known saying reminds us—history is written by the winners. Post modernity, as an indicator of cultural trauma, insists on telling the untold stories, questioning whether or not it is good or right to pursue an advancement (not just if it is possible), and deconstruction of social norms that kept people frozen in oppressive systems of power and regulation.

Cultural traumatization eventually impacts all members of society. Often it manifests in subtle ways as we relate to one another or as we perceive our own potential for flourishing and hope. As a clinician who works with many people in their 20s and early 30s, I wonder how much of the latent anxiety that haunts my clients and interferes with their lives, even when life is going well and they are achieving their goals, is a manifestation of cultural post traumatic response. It is as if the level of anxiety that inhabits our communal lives is elevated leading all of us to feel a little less secure in the world.

FIRST STEPS

The first steps in recovering from traumatizing experiences and post traumatic response is identifying and naming trauma as trauma. For many communities and individuals, including survivors, perpetrators, and loved ones, there is an inherent pull to deny the presence of traumatic wounding in our lives and communities—especially if we are participants in the infliction of traumatic wounding. Seeing, naming, and seeking to understand the harms we experience requires either tremendous courage or desperation. Nevertheless, until we acknowledge the presence of traumatic wounding we will inevitably act out of that wounded-ness.

Traumatic wounding occurs visibly, dramatically, acutely, subtly, perniciously, chronically, relationally, systemically, and across all demographic categories. Correspondingly, post traumatic responses can range from debilitating addictions to compulsions of perfection but are always a strategy for coping with tremendous stress and overwhelm. Survivors fighting through post traumatic responses are not ontologically broken, shattered, annihilated, or existentially undone; they are individuals who have been injured and still retain resources for recovery, resiliency, and restoration of health and flourishing—even if it often doesn't feel that way. Post traumatic responses impact how survivors understand themselves, relationships, and the world, and the impact of trauma in our bodies, minds, souls, and relationships is our next area of focus.

2

Impact of Trauma

Events of crisis impact individuals and communities in a variety of ways. For some, crisis events are survived, processed, and move into the past; yet, for others, these crisis events get "stuck" and induce post traumatic responses. Whether or not an individual, family, community, society, or culture intuitively processes crisis events to enough resolution or if those experiences are traumatizing depends on a great variety of factors, including those discussed in chapter 1. Ultimately, the scale shifts one way or the other depending on whether or not there is enough supportive resources internally built up prior to the crisis event/s and/or externally offered during and after the experience of crisis to facilitate processing and resolution. When the intensity of the crisis remains below the threshold of resources and coping, crisis events are generally processed by our innate resources. If the intensity of crisis is greater than our internal and external resources, overwhelm occurs and traumatization is more likely. Simply stated, it is about the ratio of vulnerability to threat of overwhelm. Additionally, the full weight of post traumatic responses and the impact of trauma may be immediately experienced if there is enough safety for processing to begin. However, the full impact of trauma may not become visible for years following the crisis event, especially in instances of chronic traumatization. In ongoing environments of violation and threat, survival often means covering up traumatic responses. If it is unsafe to express the realities of violation and harm, then continued survival requires covering over, pretending as if all is ok, or denial of the experiences of traumatic wounding. Of course the longer a person relies on their coping/covering strategies for survival, the more familiar and automatic these strategies for life become.

For clergy and persons in other helping professions, awareness of the variability of traumatic responses and survival strategies is essential for providing good, non-re-traumatizing support, including the supports of pastoral care and preaching. When we limit our vision of post traumatic response to the ways in which it manifests in particular groups (veterans, sexual assault survivors, victims of child abuse, etc.), we risk missing the signs of distress in other groups. Becoming aware of the primary features of post traumatic response as criteria for clinical diagnosis is a wonderful and necessary first step; however, clinical diagnostic criteria fail to illuminate post traumatic responses that are prosocial or subclinical. The next step is to cultivate an understanding of *how* post traumatic responses function and to what purpose.

INTERNAL FAMILY SYSTEMS AS A LENS FOR TRAUMA

In order to recognize the multivariate impacts of traumatic stimuli, it is helpful to have a framework for understanding how people are put together. The model I have found most helpful in my personal, clinical, and intellectual life is Internal Family Systems (IFS).[1] IFS is a model of psychotherapy developed by Richard Schwartz in the concluding decades of the 20th century. It is currently an evidence based practice and included in a list of preferred therapies by Bessel van der Kolk[2]. IFS is highly illuminative in conceptualizing the internal world of personal and interpersonal systems and accompanying resources in the person as well as the vulnerabilities. Additionally, it provides a framework that facilitates and embodies the four primary commitments of trauma-sensitive theology and practice: priority of the body, acceptance of lived narrative experience, recognition of natural, adaptive, healthy psychological multiplicity, and resources for and faith in resiliency. Internal Family Systems was initially derived from family systems therapy, begins with the claim that all of us have "parts," and that all parts are welcome and have an intention to help us. As discussed in the introduction, our various parts can "show up" as emotions, images, thoughts, sensations, impulses and/or a clustering of these presentations. Internal Family Systems advocates that parts generally function in one of three ways: exiles, managers, or firefighters (I refer to firefighters as "escape

1. For more information about Internal Family Systems or to inquire about training opportunities, visit www.centerselfleadership.com.

2. van der Kolk, *The Body Keeps the Score*, 277–95.

artists" in my clinical practice to emphasize the function of the group of parts and to reduce client misinterpretations. Firefights are often seen as heroic first responders and while these parts may feel heroic at the outset that is not the primary quality intended in the model).

Broadly speaking, exiles function to hold and contain our experiences of being hurt. These parts receive our experiences of trauma, fears of being "not (fill in the blank) enough," emotions that we presume are too big or threatening like shame, guilt, or anger (for some), and memories that get disconnected from the personal narrative about our life that meets the criteria of social acceptability. The categories of managers and firefighters/escape artists operate with the intention of protecting us from the hurts that are held by the exiled parts. Managers work to keep us functional and meeting the demands of life and relationship. These parts get us out of bed when we'd rather sleep in, make sure we complete our work on time, prompt us to exercise, eat healthfully, and follow laws. When in balance, managers are wonderful assets for functional living; however, when out of balance, managers can be highly critical, perfectionistic, people-pleasers, and lead us into unhealthy patterns of control. Managers get increasingly out of balance when exiles get "triggered" or activated or as a response to prolonged lack of physical or relational safety. As exiles attempt to garner more attention for care and witness, managers can perceive exile activation as a threat to social functioning and grow increasingly rigid in an attempt to maintain control. Unfortunately, managers aren't fully equipped to be the leader of our internal system and eventually get overwhelmed or exhausted in the effort to maintain functionality. When managers get exhausted and struggle to continue overfunctioning, firefighters or escape artists jump in to ease the pressure. Colloquially, these are the parts that just say "screw it, I'm done with this." Firefighters effectively put out the fire of pressure but flood the house as a result. These are the parts that seek escape through a wide range of behaviors including addictions (food, exercise, internet, alcohol, drugs), prolonged distractions (tv, computer, Netflix binging, social media), emotional outbursts, or harmful behaviors. These parts are effective in providing temporary relief from the pressure but often reactivate exiles whose needs fueled the process to begin with.

In addition to parts, IFS makes the bold claim that *all* of us also have a space within us and a dimension of who we are that IFS calls the "Self." Self is that core sense of who we are when we are able to discover our authentic being. Religious traditions utilize language of the soul, spirit, imago, etc. to refer to the place of connection between the divine and the human person. And like religious traditions, the more one tries to "nail down" exactly what the soul or Self is, the more elusive it becomes. The Self, for IFS, is experienced somatically, or in the body, by a sense and spirit of groundedness, compassion, curiosity, creativity, clarity, courage, calmness, confidence, and connection. When we sense these characteristics within us, we are accessing "Self energy." IFS takes as a given that *all* persons have a Self and that the Self remains even in the midst of life's most horrific experiences. It is always available as a resource for resilient recovery and wisdom. In cases of chronic traumatization, parts "take the hits" of traumatic wounding in protection of the Self. Rather than being "shattered," "broken," or "annihilated," the Self is covered over and protected by parts who then take on roles of increasing leadership of the person, sometimes in problematic and unhealthy ways.

Instead of trying to "get rid of" or further fix, manage, or control parts, IFS encourages us to bring compassion and curiosity to all the parts of our self. According to the IFS model, all parts have good intentions and wisdom alongside the fears that emerge from wounding. The challenge is that life often includes big and small injuries to who we are as people. When we are wounded, our parts take the wounding and form a belief or burden about the world, relationships, or our self in response to the wounding. For instance, if we experience chronic abuse or neglect as a child, an exiled part may hold a substantial fear emotion, sensation of nausea in the stomach, and the belief "I am never safe." A manager part may attempt to survive and cope by always trying to be good and perfect. This manager part could show up in perfectionism, tightness in the chest and throat, anxiety, and hold the belief "If I do everything right, then nothing bad can happen/If I ever mess up, everything will fall apart." A firefighter/escape artist part could develop that uses dissociation behaviors to check out of one's body in the midst of abuse or utilize self injury to release the pressure of always having to be perfect. These firefighter/escape artist parts may hold beliefs like "It's not safe in my body; I have to leave" or "If I'm going to get hurt, I least I'll decide how and when." IFS recognizes that parts acquire burdens through relational wounds, some of which are Traumatic in nature and others that are not big T traumatic but still result in learnings and beliefs that are ultimately unsustainable. In this model, parts aren't the "problem" and shouldn't be further ignored or exiled; rather, the challenges of life and psychological health occur when part's beliefs or strategies for living are outdated or troublesome. Through support, guidance, and the building of trust between a person's Self and parts, parts are able to gradually relax, receive care for old and new wounds, and reclaim their innate wisdom and gifts.

Internal Family Systems is a particularly rich lens for identifying, having compassion, and offering support for survivors of traumatic experience/s. IFS is built on the depathologizing of parts, facilitation of connections between parts and Self, recognition of somatic manifestations of post traumatic response, honoring the narrative experiences from the perspective of the part/s, and providing a resource via Self for resiliency and health. Many of the symptoms of post-traumatic stress disorder and other trauma related mental health concerns can be more clearly seen, held, and cared for when identified as a set of parts and the burdens held by those parts. The competing needs of requiring care and support from others with the push back away from relationships to feel safe enough can be maddening when assumed to be from a unitary personality; however, when understood as different parts who hold different learnings, fears, and burdens, it is easier to maintain a sense of compassion and balance for the demonstrated struggle to feel safe enough in relationship. Ultimately, sustainable and vivifying life emerges from a well balanced, internally compassionate, Self-led psychological system. The great resource offered by IFS is a roadmap of how to identify parts that are wounded, reconnect parts to the caring resources of Self, and facilitate robust resiliency that includes *all* parts of the person.

(POST) TRAUMATIC RESPONSE

Traumatic and post traumatic responses impact survivors biologically, somatically, psychologically, relationally, and spiritually. The fact that our experiences, mundane and extraordinary, impact who we are and how we know our self is not news. Traumatic experiences change us—though the change is remarkable in its degree rather than in its presence. As biological organisms we are always in the process of growing, expelling those things and beliefs that are no longer helpful or adaptive to our lives, and changing as a result. The noteworthy dimension of the way traumatizing events impact us is that these experiences are catalysts for change at a more intense pace and felt influence. Traumatizing experiences are tipping points that knock us off balance and demand a rethinking and a reformation of our most deeply held assumptions about our life and the world. The ripple effect of traumatic wounding begins at the time of traumatic incidence in our physiology, gets held somatically in the cells and tissues of our body, becomes stuck in our brain's mechanism for processing in full, raises questions about relationships that were insufficient in protection, and prompts wonderings about how the world works and God's role in it. The intensity of this ripple effect can range from that of a rough wave to a catastrophic tsunami.

Traditional clinical wisdom when thinking about post traumatic response is to begin with the behavioral and psychological symptoms delineated in the Diagnostic and Statistical Manual of Mental Disorders (DSM, now in its 5th edition). This approach is functional enough when a person engages a clinician seeking relief from traumatic stress symptoms. Unfortunately when we go straight to the psychological and relational manifestations of traumatic wounding, we also potentially miss caring for the biological (hormonal and neurochemical) and somatic underpinnings of traumatic injury. The intention of this section is to provide an overview of the impact of trauma biologically, somatically, psychologically, relationally, and spiritually; though this clearly will not be an exhaustive review of the impact of traumatic wounding on persons and communities.

Biological

Human beings are wired to pay more attention to experiences and objects that are novel or elicit a strong emotional response than the attention we give to every day occurrences. Everyday experiences often fade seamlessly into our daily lives and the associated memories fade quickly or blend into obscurity. The blending of daily mundane tasks is a good sign; it indicates a rhythm of life that is familiar and facilitates a feeling of safety. Evolutionarily this makes a lot of sense for enhancing survival and for maintaining a homeostasis of excitement and consistency. Novel experiences excite our brains via dopamine release and activate our sympathetic nervous system. This one of the reasons why Facebook and social media can be addictive— the elevating "need" for increasing levels of information and "connection." Novelty is exciting and when we are excited we are more alert and engaged in the moment. Likewise, we also tend to remember experiences that correspond to intense emotion, whether happy or sad, while forgetting the mundane tasks that often populate our daily lives. Experiences that elicit a strong bioemotional response stick because the memories of them are potentially more integral to our overall survival. For early humans, remembering which water sources are safe and which are occupied by predators provided a survival advantage. Knowing exactly where you were almost bitten by a serpent or alligator is an important thing to recall and having a body system that elevates attention, blood flow to your musculature, and rate of response grants you a higher likelihood of survival.

During a traumatic experience, mammals have three fundamental neurobiological system responses/options that are selected subconsciously based on the perceived degree of risk and safety.

> The level of safety determines which one of these is activated at any particular time. Whenever we feel threatened, we instinctively turn to the first level, social engagement (activation of ventral vagal complex [VVC]). We call out for help, support, and comfort from the people around us. But if no one comes to our aid, or we're in immediate danger, the organism reverts to a more primitive way to survive: fight or flight (activation of the sympathetic nervous system [SNS]). We fight off our attacker, or we run to a safe place. However, if this fails—we can't get away, we're held down or trapped—the organism tries to preserve itself by shutting down and expending as little energy as possible. We are then in a state of freeze or collapse (activation of the dorsal vagal complex [DVC]).[3]

The symptoms present as a result of unresolved trauma correspond to the survival mechanisms that are automatically employed during traumatic survival according to degree of perceived threat. The trajectory of a "normal" response to threat is: perception of threat, activation of the limbic system (the "emotional" brain) where the amygdala signals an alarm to the body, activation of the sympathetic nervous system and adrenal glands which secrete epinephrine and norepinephrine, and mobilization of the body for fight/flight with increases in adrenaline, blood flow to the arms and legs and decreased blood flow to the digestive system. When the threat is neutralized the body releases cortisol which inhibits the alarm response. When this system is permitted to complete, the organism is returned to safety and restored to biological homeostasis. In cases where post traumatic response occurs, the trajectory follows the same route up to the point of a release of cortisol to stop the alarm response. Post traumatic response

3. Van der Kolk, *Body Keeps the Score*.

occurs when the mobilization of fight/flight or freeze is ineffective to garner safety and the mobilization response continues keeping the person in an extended state of fight or flight response. Likewise, individuals living with post traumatic response also show increased levels of cortisol (the stress hormone) as the body continues to release cortisol in an effort to regain homeostasis.[4]

Traumatic stimuli overwhelm an organism's ability to respond and incorporate the experience into narrative memory. In other words, the survival mechanisms, that optimally function to keep us alive, glitch and some elements of the traumatic experience get stuck and retain a "here-and-now"quality as the event moves into the temporal past. Many of the clinical features of primary trauma responses are essentially the ghosts of adaptive survival responses. For instance, hypervigilance and activation of the SNS, in the immediacy of trauma, allows the organism to attend to a breadth of external and internal stimuli that facilitates a greater chance of survival. The ghosts of hypervigilance haunt in the form of nightmares, flashbacks, and a hypersensitive startle response. Hypo-arousal and the numbing of body sensation due to activation of the DVC at the time of trauma permit the organism to separate awareness from bodily pain allowing for either the persistence of movement to escape or to employ a freeze response that minimizes further bodily injury. The ghosts of hypo-arousal are present in dissociation. The majority of the symptoms of post-traumatic stress disorder are either a prolonged activation of survival mechanisms or attempts to minimize exposures in post trauma life to places and things that retrigger the extended survival response. Understanding the biological roots of post traumatic response is essential for caring professionals because it helps us place the symptoms of post traumatic response in a context that is compassionate and non-pathologizing. Flashbacks, and other symptoms, are not a sign of a lack of faith; rather, they are a prolongation of biological survival mechanisms past their time of utility.

Somatic

Post traumatic response is a bodily response. The body increases the presence of adrenaline, epinephrine, norepinephrine, and blood flow to the arms and legs with the intention to fight or flee a threat in order to survive. However, what happens when the fight/flight response is stalled? In many

4. Rothschild, *The Body Remembers*, 10–11.

46

different types of traumatic exposure, fighting or fleeing are not options. Children experiencing abuse from care givers can not risk fighting or running because they continue to rely on the caregiver for survival. In many cases of domestic violence or sexual assault, fighting back increases the risk of harm. Survivors of car accidents or natural disasters may be rendered physically powerless to respond actively to threat. When the fight/flight process stalls, the impulse can remain as the body moves into shut down or freeze. Sensorimotor psychotherapy, developed by Pat Ogden,[5] pays particular attention to the ways in which protective movement impulses stall or get frozen in the body. For instance, if a person is under physical threat and has the somatic impulse to punch but then, thanks to increase in vigilance, realizes that they are unlikely to physically best their attacker. The energy diverted to the musculature of the arm in order to fight may become "stuck" and show up later on as a pain in the arm or unconscious habit of making a clenched fist when under stress. Likewise, during threats the body transfers blood flow to the limbs and away from the digestive tract. When the threat response fails to neutralize and develops into post traumatic response, the survivor may notice bowel discomfort or inflammation.

Survivors of traumatic wounding often do not speak openly of the ways in which their body retains the sensations of harm, or body memories.

> "Body" memory is another term that has been used clinically to identify implicit somatic memory (Siegel, 2003). *Body memory* refers to recollections of trauma that emerge through somatic experience: muscle tension, movements, sensations, autonomic arousal, and so on . . . [T]actile sensations, internal sensations (such as trembling), kinesthetic responses (such as muscular tension), vestibular responses (such as feelings of dizziness that occur in response to trauma stimuli), and the somatic components of a defensive subsystem (such as the constriction associated with freezing) are all examples of ways in which the trauma is remembered through implicit body memories.[6]

Body memories are unfortunately too frequently neglected in our consideration of the impact of trauma. Consequently, the somatic injuries of trauma are left out of therapeutic models that focus exclusively on the cognitive dimensions of post traumatic response and can remain a challenge or place of shame and concern past "successful" processing of the cognitive

5. Ogden, *Trauma and The Body.*
6. Ibid., 237.

dimensions of traumatic wounding. For survivors of early life (under three years of age) or chronic abuse, the "story" of traumatic wounding is primarily told in body memories since the linguistic centers of the brain were not fully developed at the time of trauma exposure. At times, body memories invade awareness and disrupt life leading survivors to feel unsafe, or at least uncomfortable, in and with their body. When we fear our embodiment, we avoid knowing our bodies or inhabiting them fully and remain as strangers in our most intimate home—our body. Full, aware, embodiment is a challenge for many survivors of traumatic violation who experienced violence to their body.

Resiliency includes a care-full reclamation of inhabiting one's body. Movement practices that elevate somatic awareness, mindfulness, interoception, and attending to the inner wisdom that emerges from the body are rich resources for cultivating resiliency from traumatic wounding. Movement traditions like yoga, 5 Rhythms, Tai Chi, Nia, Feldenkrais, and communal and rhythm dances from around the world have the capacity to offer care for the remnants of traumatic wounding in the body. Each of these practices facilitates a mindful care towards the needs, impulses, and movements of the body and bodywisdom. When we can begin to reconnect back to our bodies, increase our somatic awareness, strengthen our conscious breathing, attune to the resonance of bodies, move with mindfulness according to the wisdom of our cells, and touch our own bodies[7] and share consensual loving touch with other bodies, we support resiliency from traumatic wounding.

Models of care, psychotherapy or community support, are most helpful when they welcome the body as a full participant in survival and resiliency. For clergy and communities of faith, compassionate care of the body is both a challenge and a strength. In many ways, religious rites of passage (baptism, marriage, eucharist, laying on of hands, funerals) are highly embodied. When we can care for the body as equally vital to the spirit or soul for fullness of life, we have the opportunity to generate body memories of care and acceptance.

7. Somatic awareness, conscious breathing, somatic resonance, mindful movement, and attuned touch are the five practices of Somatic Internal Family Systems developed by Susan McConnell.

Psychological

As indicated above, most of the symptoms of post-traumatic stress disorder, as one manifestation of post traumatic response, can be connected to the no longer functional extended activation of healthy and adaptive survival mechanisms. The biological systems intended to protect us from significant harm or death are overwhelmed, continue to operate the processes of threat response and lead to patterns of dysregulation (becoming chronically overstimulated/hyperaroused or understimulated/hypoaroused). In the language of IFS, there are parts that come to believe that they must always remain vigilant or on high alert in order to remain safe. And, there are other parts that keep us a little bit frozen so that we don't become overwhelmed again. Clinically, this is the language of flashbacks, increased startle response, sleep disturbances, irritability and anger, and distressing reminders or recollections, on one hand; and, on the other, decreased interest, dissociation, decrease in concentration, avoidance of places and things, and detachment from relationships. These manifestations of post-traumatic stress disorder correspond to the ways in which our psychological and somatic systems attempt to regain a sense of balance and safety but end up overshooting to one end then another. The flip flopping from one emotional or behavioral extreme to another is one way in which our psychological and somatic systems seek to recalibrate and find a new normal of life.

The psychological dimensions of post traumatic response can be frightening and disruptive for survivors and their loved ones. The great effort to re/member, to put back together as a whole the various elements of traumatic re/collection, is one of the challenges of traumatic experience. When systems of survival become overwhelmed, the visual, olfactory, tactile, auditory, emotional, proprioceptive, and kinesiological components of the experience can become separated from one another. The components of the experience that can be taken in are processed like all other memories; however, those parts of the experience that can not be taken in remain active as triggers of the crisis event. Unconsolidated sensory information remains active as a hook for flashbacks that disrupt life and pull survivors back into the past crisis event. Traumatic memories prompt needs to avoid images, smells, touches, sounds, feelings, internal sensations, movements, and body postures that call back into the present the haunting events of the past. EMDR (eye movement desensitization and reprocessing)[8] is a psy-

8. Francine Shapiro, *Getting Past Your Past*.

chotherapeutic model, theory, and technique that focuses on re/collecting the components of experience and facilitating their reconnection and full processing. EMDR offers a process that mirrors the body's natural memory processing systems to facilitate recovery from trauma.

The majority of the psychological ramifications of traumatic wounding flow out of survival mechanisms that are no longer helpful in the present. The intention of post traumatic response is always to facilitate survival and return the organism to safety. A return to safety can take a very long time in cases of chronic abuse and systemic oppression. The psychological resources that enable bodily survival of threat and violation also generate an internal distance from Self as protection. The internal distance of the psyche from the sensation of the body facilitates survival of the crisis event by desensitizing one to pain or by creating a separation that allows the Self to be protected and held in trust. When we can understand the challenges issued by post traumatic psychological response as a prolonged resource of survival rather than as a sign of brokenness that indicates future potential, we can more clearly see the processes at work in the psychological impact of traumatization. And, when we can see more clearly, we can respond more compassionately and authentically with resources and paths of hope for resilient recovery.

Relational

Human beings are social and relational creatures. We come into being and thrive when we are in healthy relationships and community. I recall a professor in my clinical master's program describing babies as inextricably linked to mommies. In her description of the infant psyche she states on behalf of the baby, "Mommy and I are one and I'm the one." Her intention was to highlight how we, as human beings, are in relationship even before we draw our first breath. It is true that human infants are utterly dependent on caregivers to meet all of our survival needs for a much longer duration than other mammals. It is also true that infants are completely dependent on their mothers for emotional regulation and identity formation.[9] When an infant receives "good enough"[10] care, support, and mirroring from primary caregivers, they begin to form secure attachments to others. Secure attachments in early life provide the foundation for healthy adult relation-

9. Allan Shore, *Affect Regulation and the Origin of the Self.*

10. "Good enough" is a reference to D. Winnicott and his notion of the "good enough mother."

ships later in life and a sense of being ok enough in the world. When care is not "good enough" via neglect, inconsistency, or harm, patterns of inse-cure attachments form (avoidant, anxious, or disorganized). These three attachment styles, avoidant, anxious, and disorganized, are all indicative of uncertainty and a sense of a lack of sufficient safety in early life.

> People who possess a secure attachment style tend to develop mental models of themselves as being friendly, good-natured, and likeable and of significant others as being generally well inten-tioned, reliable, and trustworthy. Those who display an anxious style tend to develop models of themselves as being misunder-stood, unconfident, and underappreciated and of significant oth-ers as being typically unreliable and either unwilling or unable to commit themselves to permanent relationships. And those who have an avoidant style typically develop models of themselves as being suspicious, aloof, and skeptical and of significant others as being basically unreliable or overly eager to commit themselves to relationships.[11]

Persons with a disorganized attachment style develop behaviors characterized by a push and pull dynamic of relationships. When offered reunion with a significant other, those with a disorganized attachment may initially run towards the other then emotionally shut down, hit, start an argument, or back away.

Attachment theory was first offered by John Bowlby and expanded by Mary Ainsworth. Ainsworth's the "Strange Situation" test first recognized the connection between attachment responses in young children and pres-ence of trauma or neglect in early life. Viewed through the lens of post traumatic responses, it is of little surprise that children who experience the world as safe enough, compassionate enough, and sufficiently meeting one's needs would grow with an understanding of a good enough self, par-ent, society, and world. On the other hand, those children who experience their early world as lacking, hostile, uncertain, or neglectful would grow up with a psychosomatic system wired to survive in an environment of trau-ma. Anxious attachments are quite reminiscent of hyper-arousal responses to trauma. Avoidant attachments mirror the detachment of hypo-arousal. And, disorganized attachments reveal the inner tug of war resulting from an internal system that is stuck in internal polarity. Secure attachments, by contrast, illuminate how relationships can operate when each person

---

11. Simpson, "Influence of Attachment Styles," 971–80.

is internally balanced with a deep trust in the sufficiency of one's internal resources and trust in the sustainability of the world and society.

Attachment theory is really helpful for recognizing how different people relate with one another and in illuminating the impact of early abuse or neglect on the person. Recognition is important because it gives survivors and care givers a lens for understanding what is going on in relationships and a starting place for recovery. Illumination is important because it reveals the importance of social bonding and care in the midst and immediate aftermath of crisis events. As you will recall, the first course of action that human beings take when in need of help is to call for social support, activation of the ventral vagal complex. We call out vocally for help, our eyes widen, our facial expression shifts to indicate desperation, our bodies move to draw attention in solicitation of response from others. The activation of the social network in times of need is the first choice for those with secure attachments (and for infants). If social support fails, we go into fight/flight mode and activation of the SNS. This second level of response is indicative of anxious attachment styles and reveals both the failure of social support and the elevation of the internal alarm system. On a larger scale, I am reminded of the anger that can occur after natural disasters when survivors of disaster experience the lack of care by the larger society as a betrayal and abandonment. The avoidant attachment style parallels the activation of the dorsal vagal complex that results in the freeze or shut down response in trauma survivors. This attachment style is fundamentally an indicator of disengagement from and a lack of hope in relationships. Finally, disorganized attachment styles are illuminative of active post traumatic response which vacillates between increasingly extreme responses.

While there is a tendency to identify attachment styles as a static way of being, how we attach with others and to the various dimensions of who we are internally, to our parts, can be altered either for the better with experiences that help facilitate more secure relationships or towards greater struggle with continued experiences of violation or neglect. One of the fundamental and essential characteristics of the psychotherapeutic relationship is to create and foster a relational dynamic that is attuned, compassionate, nonjudgmental, congruent, authentic, and safe. The literature on what makes therapy effective regularly finds that the durability and quality of the therapeutic alliance is a stronger indicator of effectiveness than any other feature, including techniques utilized or school of thought. Simply stated, it is the relationship that matters the most. When we can foster opportunities for people to experience secure relationships of care, we facilitate resiliency and health.

Spiritual

The relational attachments that we develop first with our primary caregiver set the template for future relationships with loved ones and how we negotiate our social world. Additionally, our early attachments inform our attachments to the divine and the ways in which we confess our relationship with the divine presence that finds expression in the world's religions and spirituality forms. If we are secure in our experience of love and sustenance, our theological confessions and spiritual practices will reflect our secure attachment. If we experience our primary caregiver as neglectful or abusive, then our anxious or avoidant attachment style will be revealed in our sense of the divine as neglectfully absent or oppressively powerful. Our theology and spirituality always reflects our experiences of security or of neglect/abuse either in a direct correlation or in an overcorrective reversal. The dynamic flow of experience to theology is not unidirectional; it is circular. Just as our experiences inform our spirituality, our spirituality also informs the way we interpret our experiences. God or the divine, however you conceive of it, can be a sturdy, robust resource for resiliency—a steady center point in the midst of the chaos of trauma. Faith can support survivors in the journey of recovery; however, unhealthy faith and theology can increase the injury sustained by trauma. It goes both ways.

There are few experiences in life that can prompt a crisis of faith like experiences of crisis events, traumatizing or non-traumatizing. Crisis events, whether the event is the sudden death of a loved one, the destruction of a home by weather or fire, the diagnosis of a terminal disease, assault or bodily violation, or presence in war, cause us to question our understanding of the world and the divine. Questions of "why?" reverberate into our cells and through every belief that felt the quake of crisis. For those who hold a more traditional Christian theology, these crisis of faith moments are encapsulated in the question of theodicy: "If God is good and all powerful, then how is there suffering and evil in the world?" The theological equation just doesn't work as it stands. The realization that the core presuppositions of faith are inadequate in providing clarity of meaning or support in the face of traumatizing crisis events is, for many people, part of what makes traumatizing crisis events so destabilizing. For survivors of crisis events, the experience of post traumatic response can also challenge one's faith. Questions like "where was God when. . . ?" have the capacity to haunt survivors.

PIECING TOGETHER RESILIENCY

Traumatizing experience/s and event/s unquestionably impact survivors in a multitude of ways. The impact of trauma sends shock waves that reverberate throughout most areas of life and self awareness. It does shake and threaten to undo and feels like a shattering of everything that once felt solid and stable. The aftermath of trauma is hard and messy and ugly. However, it is not the end of the story. Resiliency and recovery from traumatic wounding and post traumatic response is possible; yet, it does require awareness, courage, and knowledge. Resiliency and recovery require awareness of the full scope of wounding. Trauma impacts the biology, body, mind, relationships, and spirit. Resources to facilitate recovery must take into account all of the ways in which wounding occurs. Resiliency requires courage to face the full depths of injury and the weight of harm. Caring for post traumatic response, in oneself or as a support for another, and journeying through traumatic processing is not for the faint of heart. It is a difficult and daunting path *and* it is a path that does travel through as long as you keep going. As I remind my clients, there is no way around, only through. Pretending the wounds aren't there only makes them worse, like a physical wound that gets infected and becomes a growing threat to survival of the person. The path through is difficult because it requires a re/membering and re/collection. This journey is necessary to reach a place of authenticity, health, and fullness of life. And, it requires courage. Resiliency requires knowledge of what happens in traumatic wounding. When we seek to walk with others through the path of post traumatic response, trauma processing, and resiliency, we must stay informed. Knowledge requires us to continue to learn about the ways in which trauma impacts persons and communities. For clergy and theologians, being knowledgeable means cultivating the humility to realize that most of us operate with a tragically thin traumatology that can put us at risk of inflicting harm. Awareness, courage, and knowledge are a few of the first steps for constructing a trauma-sensitive theology and practice that can facilitate resiliency.

3

Cultivating Practices
of Resiliency after Trauma

ostering post traumatic processing and resiliency requires care for mind, body, and spirit. Care of mind has traditionally be the focal point of psychotherapeutic intervention; however, as research into traumatic wounding, post traumatic response, and resiliency increasingly discovers, care of body and care of spirit are of equal importance to care of mind. Awareness, compassion, and understanding of traumatic wounding and the journey towards resiliency lead us to practices of care in our thinking, speaking, rituals, and communities. In order for recovery and resiliency to be complete, holistic care requires inclusion of care of the body, restoration of connections in community, and reclamation of relationship with the divine in whatever form resonates with the individual. Congregational leaders and care providers are uniquely suited to provide meaningful adjunctive support to psychotherapeutic interventions and are perhaps better equipped than mental health care providers to foster connections and attachments among survivors, community, and the divine.

ROLES OF COMMUNAL LEADERSHIP TOWARDS RESILIENCY

Religious leaders and care providers have two primary roles in the care of persons who have survived trauma: adjunct to professional mental health care and primary in cultivating spaces and communities of safety and care. The role of clergy as adjuncts to professional care by mental health professionals has been discussed in various ways in preceding chapters. The important points to remember at this juncture are the need for training about post traumatic response, a network of professionals to function as referral partners, and intentionality regarding interpretation and proclamation of scripture and theology. Providing adjunct support to those recovering from traumatic wounding can be an honorable opportunity to witness a person's profound capacity for both struggle and resiliency. Journeying with survivors of traumatic wounding can reveal both the tenuousness of our vulnerability, the fierceness of our fight for survival and desire for fullness of life. Being granted the honor of witnessing the profound vulnerability and resiliency of the human person and community can provide a window into our understanding of the divine and inform our theological anthropology in ways that few other life experiences offer.

In addition to this role as adjunct support, clergy can also function as a primary care provider by modeling and embodying leadership for resiliency by providing care for community so that our communities are spaces for safe and healthy relational attachments. One of the two primary ways in which clergy can cultivate communities of faith that are safe attachment partners for people who have experienced traumatic wounding is to model a leadership and way of being that is open, compassionate, courageous, and curious. When we are able to provide grounding compassionate care for the wounding within our own lives and for the non-traumatic wounds in our community we generate a space that is more capable of holding survivors of traumatic experience/s with congruence, grace, and care.

A second avenue for clergy to function as a primary care provider is as curator of meaningful ritual process that connect human beings with the divine. Two of the enduring strengths of communities of faith are as holders of rituals that mark and midwife us through life's significant milestones and as home of communities that hopefully embody the qualities of life, empathy, and love. Rituals function across cultures as rites of passage that provide stability, meaning, and recognition of the myriad of ways in which we move from "befores," through the liminal space of "betwixt and between,"[1] and emerge into a new "now" as it truly is including all of the incumbent challenges and promises alike. For individuals and communities who have experienced traumatic wounding, there is a clear distinction between life "before" and life "now." Traumatic wounding changes things and there is no going back to the "before." While one can never "go back," rituals

1. Van Gennep, *Rites of Passage*.

can facilitate the movement from wounding to resiliency if conducted with intentional care and compassionate holding by a community.

The two avenues of primary care readily available for clergy, communities, and survivors can be wisely dovetailed. The combination of healthy community attachment and rituals that provide meaning, witness, and structure is a powerful offering to facilitate resiliency and recovery from traumatic wounding. While it is imperative to maintain the distinctions between therapeutic modalities and techniques for trauma processing and the community rituals that can assist with attachment and meaning making, there are elements of post-traumatic therapeutic processing that can be incorporated into existing rituals to make them more beneficial. Intentional and mindful incorporation of therapeutic elements that draw on traditions of somatic awareness and wisdom do not require a replacement of elements of established rituals; rather, many of these elements are already present, as intuited by the efficacy of rituals throughout history, and just need highlighting as significant components rather than adiaphora.

RECLAIMING SOMATIC WISDOM

Reclaiming and highlighting the practices of somatic wisdom necessary to cultivate spiritual practices of processing traumatic wounding and promoting resiliency are challenged by the normative strain of western Christianity that has a long history of denigrating somatic wisdom and naming the body as an enemy of faith and spirituality. The demonization of the body as a deceiver and locus of sin has rendered human persons from our most innate wisdoms and compounded the shame associated with traumatic wounding. Before communities of faith can step fully into their roles as supporters of resiliency and fullness of life, we must come to terms with the ways in which we have traumatically rendered body from spirit. Body or somatic wisdom includes attention to all of the human senses, personal and communal intuition, and an intentional re-weaving of sensation and intuition into the life of worship and communities of faith. Re-establishing worship and the practices of communal life as a home to the fullness of embodied, incarnate human being requires us to renew the honor of an epistemology of sensation. In all other areas of life, we depend on the wisdom of our sensory system to know the world, our current place within it, and to negotiate potential risks. However, and especially for those of us within the Protestant Christian tradition, religious spaces reserve the senses of hearing and sight (with taste only minimally utilized in the rite of Eucharist) as means of participation with the Holy with our other senses nearly exiled from our corporate and personal spiritual practices. We read and hear the reading of holy texts and view the movement of liturgists. We employ the sense of taste when partaking of the Eucharist, though too many communities trade robust flavors of the bread for the convenience of nearly tasteless wafers. Few Protestant communities of faith utilize the tradition of burning incense thus honoring the olfactory system as a means of encountering divine presence and enhancing the mental and spiritual health of those present.[2] The gift of touch and tactile sensation is also minimized as physical contact among worshipers is reduced to handshakes in passing of the peace. Meanwhile, our kinesthetic, proprioceptive, and interoceptive sensation which undergirds our felt sense and notion of intuition are dismissed rather than being understood as simply attending to that "still small voice" of divine presence and wisdom in our lives.

Spiritual and religious practices and rituals have the capacity to heal rather than expand the breach between our physical body/somatic wisdoms and our hyper rational minds and/or disembodied spirits. However, this shift in healing the breach rather than contributing to its expansion does not happen automatically. If we continue to distance somatic wisdoms, to deny the importance of the body as a resource for health, and pass over the essence of our being as fully incarnated we perpetuate the cultural underpinnings that make recovery from traumatic wounding more difficult. Fullness of life and resiliency from traumatic wounding must include all dimensions of our being: spirit, Self, body, emotion, rationality, relationality, faith, head, heart, gut, sensation, and movement. It is folly to continue our attempt to reside out of balance, ignoring the full dimensions of all the various parts of our being. Intentional and appropriate uses of the vast traditions and rituals of the church can facilitate recovery and full, authentic life when they are deepened by an honoring of all forms of bodily sensation, attuned resonance to the Holy, and communal presence of the divine and others, and formation of communities committed to forming a web of healthy and safe attachments that can nourish and support all members.

Renewed attention to and enthusiastic embrace of the full array of sensory, kinesthetic, and relational dimensions already present in our rituals of life and faith are the first step in enhancing established ritual practices. Religious and spiritual professionals and care givers have an opportunity

2. Baldwin, *Sensing Sacred.*

to cultivate communities of faith and intentional ritual and spiritual practices that can offer a soothing balm to the injuries of traumatic wounding and response. Relationships with each other, the divine, and within ourself have the potential to reconnect us with the source of health and healing resources and energy. The intentional and appropriate use of practices of the church can facilitate recovery from traumatic wounding and traumatic response in novel and important ways distinctive of psychotherapeutic modalities; however, it doesn't always happen automatically. Rituals, communities, and spiritual practices attuned to the dynamics of traumatic wounding, response, and recovery process require care and cultivation as well as an openness to continuing learning and incorporating the wisdoms gleaned by professional work outside of the church or faith community. Restorative community care and ritual practices do not essentially need a total overhaul; rather, in order to function as an adjunctive support to clinical treatment and one resource of primary support in connection to healthy attachment and ritual processes that facilitate movement through life's most impactful moments, religious community and spiritual practices simply need to attune to the key dimensions of existing practices that already promote resiliency and amplify those dimensions. Attuning to the presence of the divine in our midst, the resources for care and support available in community, and the grounding, centering presence within each one of us are avenues towards resiliency and recovery from wounding, traumatic and non-traumatic.

BUILDING BLOCKS OF RESILIENCY

In order for religious and spiritual leaders to be mindful agents of resiliency promotion, it is imperative to have a clear understanding of the different dimensions that contribute to resiliency. The American Psychological Association defines resiliency as "the process of adapting well in the face of adversity, trauma, tragedy, threats or significant sources of stress—such as family and relationship problems, serious health problems, or workplace and financial stressors." They continue "research has shown that resilience is ordinary, not extraordinary. People commonly demonstrate resilience . . . Being resilient does not mean that a person doesn't experience difficulty or distress. Emotional pain and sadness are common in people who have suffered major adversity or trauma in their lives. In fact, the road to resilience is likely to involve considerable emotional distress."[3] All human beings have the capacity for resiliency—though not all begin with access to the same internal or external resources needed to more fully "bounce back."

A person's degree of resiliency is related to the promotive or protective factors present in their life. These factors include a person's *assets* and *resources*. An individual or community's assets are internal positive features including good enough self esteem, a felt sense of being safe in the world and "enough" (good enough, smart enough, safe enough, loved enough, etc.), self-efficacy, personal agency, etc. Resources are the external positive features in life including social support, mentors, enough material resources to meet basic needs and safety, etc.[4] The ability to identify and name internal and external protective factors is important for those who offer care and those who accept care. For those offering care, it is important to hold the awareness or remembrance of assets and resources on behalf of the survivor especially during the periods of recovery in which post traumatic response is most overwhelming. Traumatic experience, as you recall, is an experience that in those moments overwhelmed the protective factors. Consequent to traumatic overwhelm it is understandable that some parts of a community or individual may not have much hope that protective factors can help towards resiliency and may resist placing much trust in the very dimensions of internal or social life that were overwhelmed and failed to maintain safety and stability in the face of threat.

The assets and resources available as promotive factors can vary significantly from person to person or community to community. They are generally both a reflection and generative of the family systems and community that form us as individuals. They are reflective in that our early and formative attachments set our default relational paradigms. When we are formed in "good enough" families and communities with a baseline relational style that is supportive, nurturing, and secure in both resources and adaptability, we are more likely to approach our experiences with an underlying belief in support, nurturance, and securing. When we are formed in families and/or communities that struggle for stability, safety, support, and/or "enough," we are more likely to be challenged to our adaptive limits during experiences of significant threat or crisis. Likewise, if individuals or communities can identify and access dimensions of themselves that retain awareness of the qualities of care, compassion, courage, curiosity, clarity,

---

3. American Psychological Association, "What is Resilience?"

4. Zimmerman, "Resiliency Theory," 381–83.

and capability, those qualities can then assist in generating communities of resourceful nurturance. As individuals who are aware of the multiplicity within our own being, we have the capacity to offer our self and our community courageous care in the midst of potentially traumatizing adversity. The internal assets and external resources that are identified as protective factors from traumatic wounding and seeds for resilient growth are present in each of us, even when seemingly obscured by traumatic wounding and overwhelm.

When taking stock of the assets and resources available to an individual or community it is important to remain mindful that the discrepancy of promotive factors found at the community level can be correlated with systemic oppression and prevalence of intergenerational and societal traumatization. Communities of persons who have a long and intergenerational history marked by traumatic wounding and the rendering of relationships and attachment due to systems of violence (genocide of Indigenous Nations, slavery, internment or concentration camps, etc.) and the legacies of violence (heightened rates of addictions, domestic violence, poverty, incarceration, etc.) generally have access to fewer external resources and may have access to fewer internal assets. Acknowledging instances in which promotive factors are limited is not intended to further limit or discount the potential for resiliency; rather it is intended to provide space for clear acknowledgment of the situation and to encourage even more attentive care with regard to non-typical assets and resources. For instance, Native spiritual traditions, rituals, movement practices, songs, or environmental connection are avenues for support in fostering resiliency that are typically neglected by the lenses of dominant cultural forms and paths towards health.

Religious and spiritual professionals have a unique vantage point in assessing the health, with correlate strengths and challenges, of communities when given lenses that highlight the dynamics operating within internal or external grouping. As leaders of community, one of the overarching responsibilities of religious professionals is to keep tabs on the relational health of their community. While there are a variety of metrics and theoretical lenses available to assess the health of a community, few specifically include an assessment of the assets and resources available that promote resiliency. Nevertheless, this form of assessment is a key component in forming a clear vision of the health of community and capacity of the community to foster, maintain, and offer restorative relational attachments and ritual practices that promote resiliency rather than cause additional injury.

Once we begin to identify, honor, and utilize our assets and resources, we become more capable of intentionally building the foundation and path of resiliency and recovery from traumatic wounding. Three key building blocks of resiliency and recovery are a reclamation of safe sensation and body positivity, establishing safe enough relational attachments and community, and raising self esteem and agency. As indicated in a previous subsection, one of the first steps of supporting resiliency is to explicitly, in practice and preaching, reclaim the vital role of multivariate sensation and honoring of the body. Our body is our primary means of attunement and resonance—of attuning to the presence of God and the divine in our midst and resonating, thanks to our mirror neurons which facilitate empathy, with the affective states of others.

Traumatic wounding often disconnects affect, sensation, and cognitive narrative formation in the process of memory consolidation. The consequence of this disconnection are the features of traumatic response, presence of "triggers," and cultivation of behavior patterns of avoidance and self limitation. Reconnection of affect, sensation, and narrative assist in the reclamation of all parts of one self. When each of us is able to know all the dimensions of who we are more fully, we are then able to accept the multidimensionality of others with empathy and nurturance resulting in more healthy relationships and secure relational attachments and move forward in life with more confidence and courage. Right relationship with bodyself, others, and the divine facilitates and indicates robust resiliency.

COMPONENT PRACTICES TO PROMOTE RESILIENCY

Once we become aware of the components needed to support resiliency in the aftermath of disruption and trauma, the question then shifts to "how?" How can religious leaders and spiritual care professionals make intentional use of the resources already prevalent within our traditions to contribute to recovery from traumatic wounding? How do we borrow from the wisdoms of therapeutic interventions without venturing outside our scope of care? How should the practices of the church or spiritual disciplines engage with trauma recovery or is this really outside the realm of responsibility for religious leaders? Given the prevalence and variety of experiences of trauma (primary, secondary, intergenerational, societal, cultural), there is a high likelihood that survivors of traumatic experience are present in each instance of religious gatherings. Each holy-day, survivors of trauma gather in our communities to make sense of their experience/s in the world. As already indicated, experiences of traumatic overwhelm are far more common than generally acknowledged and generate questions that span all dimensions of personal understanding, interpersonal connections and relationality, and divine intention and agency. Survivors of traumatic experience grapple with the questions initiated as a consequence of trauma in every nation, congregation, synagogue, healing circle, and dinner table. To neglect the presence of trauma induced questioning and the consequent spiritual exploration hoping for a path to resiliency would be a failure of congregational care and leadership. So, how do attentive, aware, and compassionate leaders with an intention to meet the needs of survivors of all forms of traumatic exposure and response craft healthy communities and congregational gatherings that have the potential to facilitate resiliency and recovery from traumatic response?

Bessel van der Kolk is widely considered the leading expert in traumatology and care. In his text, *The Body Keeps the Score*, van der Kolk offers several "paths to recovery," therapeutic interventions for the care and treatment of trauma exposure and response.[5] The interventions Van der Kolk recommends for facilitating trauma resolution and resiliency include mindfulness, finding language (verbal or nonverbal), Eye Movement Desensitization and Reprocessing (EMDR), yoga, Internal Family Systems (IFS), neurofeedback, and communal rhythms and theater. Rather than emphasizing the conventional pattern of phase oriented treatment (safety and resource building, processing, integration into life) as the starting place for thinking about trauma treatment, Van der Kolk centers on the various components of traumatic response and the interventions that more intuitively and objectively care for each component. While EMDR, IFS, trauma-sensitive yoga, and neurofeedback each require significant professional training beyond the academic requirements to become a licensed mental health provider and should not be offered by individuals who are not trained in these modalities, they do each provide a window in to ways of supporting different dimensions of traumatic response that can be helpful when imagining ways in which communities of faith and spiritual practice can assist rather than hinder the process of resiliency and recovery from traumatic wounding. With that intention, let's devote a bit of attention to each modality.

5. Van der Kolk, *Body Keeps the Score*, 203–347.

EMDR, developed by Francine Shapiro, is an eight-phase therapeutic technique with accompanying holistic model for understanding why and how dimensions of traumatic experience remain unprocessed and continue to generate suffering. EMDR primarily focuses on the cognitive/memory component of traumatic wounding and acknowledges that during experiences of crisis or traumatic overwhelm various dimensions of experience (sensation, images, thoughts, belief about one self, affect/emotion) can be left out of our natural memory consolidation process. During non-traumatizing events, our brain inherently collects all of the pieces of our day to day experience, consolidates them, and then stores them within our memory while we sleep, generally this is believed to be a function of REM sleep. The natural cognitive processing innate in mammals is interrupted and ruptured in cases of traumatic overwhelm causing dimensions of the experience to be left out of the consolidation process. EMDR intentionally mimics the mind's inherent memory consolidation process while adding an element of conscious intention. During sleep, we do not have the capacity to choose which dimensions of experience are included or excluded in processing. However, through the process of EMDR, clinicians and clients can intentionally bring all dimensions of an experience into awareness and jump start the natural memory consolidation and procession mechanism via bilateral stimulation, alternating activation of both hemispheres of the brain. Bilateral stimulation is primarily initiated by eye movements, auditory tones, or tactile sensation alternating from left to right. The combination of bringing all dimensions of a memory into awareness paired with bilateral stimulation facilitates a more adaptive processing of the experience of traumatic overwhelm and wounding.

As researchers and clinicians continue to expand understanding and awareness of the impact and reach of traumatic experience and response on the body, mind, and soul of survivors, it is increasingly clear that any therapeutic intervention must address a wide range of symptoms and systems. It is no longer enough to only address a single dimension or area of life. While EMDR primarily attends to the multidimensionality of memory formation and consolidation, other modalities center care on the body. Trauma-sensitive yoga (TSY) is one example of a body-centered treatment avenue.[6] TSY is a therapeutic intervention that differs from more ubiquitous mat based yoga. TSY is generally chair based, invitational rather than directive, and focuses more on the interoceptive sensations than performance

---

6. David Emerson, *Trauma-Sensitive Yoga in Therapy*.

of a specific body shape or pose. In most yoga classes in the United States, classes are structured and directed by an instructor who leads the students through a series of prescribed poses with specific instructions on how to perform the poses, connect movement through poses with breath, and focused attention or mindfulness towards the breath cycle in relation to the pose with few stated invitations to discontinue the sequence or move at a different rate if desired. In TSY, the clinician offers the client an opportunity to explore a "form," if desired and when ready, with the intention of focusing attention exclusively on internal sensation of muscle activation and relaxation within the body. The intention is to help survivors of trauma connect more fully and safely with their body. For survivors whose experience of trauma included violation of bodily autonomy and consent, survival often includes distancing one's self from the experience of body violation. The survival strategy of generating disconnection to the body can make the task of inhabiting the body post-trauma extremely challenging. The aim of TSY is to reconnect survivors of trauma to their body sensation and somatic awareness in a gentle way that honors the need of survivors to assert agency and choice with regard to their body.

Internal Family Systems (IFS) is represented and discussed at multiple points within this text as model for our larger exploration and reflection. As a therapeutic intervention, two primary points of IFS are important in distinguishing it from other trauma resolution models, including models discussed here. The first point of distinction, perhaps most engaging from the perspective of religious professionals and spiritual leaders and caregivers, is the full assertion and belief in the "Self" of each person. The Self, according to IFS, is the authentic, unburdened, connected essence of a person. It is functionally "true me" without all the defenses and protections that we accumulate through living in a flawed world. Self is the wellspring within each person of resiliency and full wisdom. Self does not get shattered, broken, annihilated, or exiled; rather, Self always remains present to and within each person—though often covered by burdened and wounded protective parts. The second point of distinction is the claim that all parts of a person are welcomed and have a positive intention for our life. Some parts do take on strategies that are harmful or unaccepted by society; however, in IFS, those parts are not to be eliminated and further vilified but welcomed, understood, cared for, and ultimately unburdened so that they can resume their original, pre-wounded, place within our being. Trust in the wise presence of Self combined with acceptance of all parts of a person allows the dynamics of the clinical work to shift from the conventional phase oriented model, which reinforces parts that utilize pro-social strategies while further exiling or wounding parts that use strategies that are problematic in the long run, to a pattern that recognizes and honors the non-linear complexity of how we develop psychologically and relationally.

As discussed in the chapter on the impact of trauma, experiences of traumatic wounding impact all dimensions of life, including the ways in which our nervous system responds to stress. During experiences of prolonged or chronic traumatic overwhelm and wounding, our nervous systems have the capacity to alter our natural "default" in which moments of acute stress are met with elevated biological responses and then return to a relaxed state once the threat has passed. But what happens when the threat doesn't pass? In cases of extended threat, our nervous system has the remarkable capacity to adapt to environments in which safety is fleeting or unstable. Alterations in heart rate variability, the ability of our cardiovascular system to change the amount of time between heart beats and correspond respiration to heart beat, and brain waves, difficulty in shifting among degrees of alert and relaxed, are two of the biological and neurological shifts that correspond with symptoms of post-traumatic stress disorder. Additionally, many people who experience traumatic overwhelm and who utilized the freeze/dorsal ventral nervous system response in order to survive struggle to regain sensed connection with their body. The disconnect of awareness from sensation makes it difficult to even notice elevations of heart rate or shifts in neural activation. Biofeedback and neurofeedback training are specific body awareness interventions intended to help individuals reconnect their awareness to their internal body sensation through the use of devices that measure heart rate or brain waves and then present objective measures. In other words, these interventions provide external objective cues that mirror internal biological rhythms to help the survivor reconnect to their own interoception and somatic awareness.

The final intervention highlighted by van der Kolk is communal rhythms and theater. Just as a person's internal cardiovascular and neurological rhythms can be thrown off by traumatic wounding, our relational rhythms can be disrupted as well. These relational rhythms include one's ability to accurately "read" nonverbal body movements and facial expressions that facilitate attunement and connection, connect with the variety of internal and somatic emotional cues that help undergird empathy, and join in with the communal rituals that cohere social grouping. The experience of becoming "out of synch" or rhythm with those around us leads to an increasing sense of being misunderstood and of isolation. Social arrhythmia is both caused by and contributes to further trauma and social alienation. Finding where one can fit once again within community is an essential feature of facilitating recovery and resiliency. Theater, and other venues of embodied, narrative centered, engaged participation, provide an established structure with clear boundaries for safe and acceptable behavior that make it secure enough for people to begin to explore a fuller range of emotional and somatic feeling.

Each of the five interventions described require some degree of professional training to offer in their true form. That said and honored, it is possible to identify key benefits to each model and imagine how those features could be already present in the life and practices of our communities of faith. EMDR, at its most basic conceptualization, seeks to hold all dimensions of an experience together with awareness of echoes of experience in the past, present, and hoped for future while engaging bilateral activation in the brain. Directed attention to all dimensions of experience includes cognition, sensation, emotions, images, and narratives. How might we intentionally fill out our narratives to amplify sensory experience? Where in our communal gatherings do we utilize motion or tactile alternation? TSY offers us a lens into the importance of somatic awareness combined with an invitational rather than directive leadership. How would we imagine inviting those gathered to bring awareness to our own body experience? IFS calls to renewed faith in the core goodness and resiliency present in all living creatures at the same time that we clearly acknowledge, with curiosity, compassion, courage, creativity, and calmness, the many parts of us as individuals who all have experienced some measure of hope and wounding through life. Biofeedback and neurofeedback illuminate the internal biological rhythms that act like a rudder to a ship in steering our relational life. When we are out of synch in our own bodily being, it is more difficult to feel okay in the world. Finally, like the theater which provides participants with an opportunity to "try on" different character experiences and emotions, try out alternative response patterns, and choreograph movement, gestures, and words, religious communities can offer parallel opportunities for survivors to rediscover their social rhythms through vivid retelling of holy narratives, embodied participation in the ritual of liturgy, and the shared rhythmic cadence of songs, prayers, and creed. Each of the therapeutic interventions points us to a different dimension of traumatic wounding and a path forward towards resiliency.

SPIRITUAL PRACTICES AND DISCIPLINES

As religious and/or spiritual leaders and care providers, we are not called or equipped to function as psychotherapists; and, we have a whole wealth of resources and opportunities that are uniquely available to us as the care tenders of soul and body. Each of the world's religions and spiritualties have a host of practices and disciplines that are cultivated with an intention towards fostering health and connection to the divine (in whatever way is meaningful to the practitioners). From drum circles, yoga, and labyrinths to liturgical incense, meditation, or prayer, religious practices have functioned as key components in the community's mental, spiritual, and physical wellbeing for centuries. The ancient wisdoms and practices that infuse and support religious practices and spiritual disciplines included many of the features we are now utilizing in the care of trauma. Becoming mindful and intentional about incorporating resources for trauma resolution and resiliency is less about introducing new or strange elements into our communal life and more about reclaiming the wisdoms we have either forgotten or abandoned. The wisdoms offered by therapeutic practices of trauma care and areas to hold in remembrance as we turn to the practices and disciplines of faith are a renewed intention towards vivifying the role of full sensation, holding all dimensions of experience as important and valued, honoring the innate connection to God and the divine in each person's Self, providing care for the wounding and acceptance for all parts, returning balance to our internal biorhythms, inviting focused, mindful attention to somatic awareness, and joining with others in corporate rhythmic attunement. While there are many spiritual disciplines that can be helpful for the care of traumatic wounding in congregations, the following discussion will center on three: the practice of liturgical incense and aroma, the discipline of prayer and meditation, and an overarching view of the process of ritual practice (while remaining mindful of the great variety of rituals that all fall into the general movements of ritual practice, including ritual meals, weddings, funerals, and rites of communal initiation).

The use of incense in the worship practices of religious communities has an extended and expansive history. The burning of incense has accompanied worship practices and prayer across many religious traditions, including Buddhism, Christianity, Hinduism, Judaism, Native American Spiritual traditions, African religious traditions, and Paganism, since at least 200 BCE. While the specific form, intention, and substance differs from tradition to tradition based on the indigenous plants available to make incense and the theo-spiritual practice the use of incense accompanies, there is a clear indication that many of the world's seekers of connection to God have found the use of incense to be a helpful resource for opening up points of attachment while also providing a felt sense of healthy grounding. Unfortunately, within many forms of Protestant Christian worship, the use of incense in worship has been significantly curtailed or entirely dismissed along with other dimensions of practice that engage sensory activation and somatic awareness. The casting aside of practices that offer focused engagement of the senses and somatic awareness of introception has the high potential in curtailing our avenues for a felt sense of connection to the divine. Reclaiming the practice and/or significance of the use of incense as a vehicle in religious worship and spiritual practices can offer a variety of benefits in supporting survivors of traumatic wounding. Most generally, the intentional addition and activation of any sensory component to worship and prayer fills out another dimension of our experience in holy community and directs our awareness to our body life in the midst of worship. Many of the components of liturgical incense (frankincense, myrrh, rose, and sandalwood) have more recently been found to have therapeutic benefits for anxiety and depression as well as facilitating a sense of wellbeing. Additionally, the addition of oils that support traumatic response such as neroli (*Citrus aurantium var. amara*) or patchouli (*Pogostemom cablin*) can support and soothe experiences of traumatic overwhelm and dissociation, respectively, when added to incense already in use by the community. The primary shift I am advocating is to see the practice of the use of incense in worship as an intentional decision on the part of religious leaders to support the somatic awareness, sensory engagement, and symptoms of trauma response of participants in the worship or prayer experience.

The practice of calming and centering one's mind and body with the intention of connecting in either felt presence or communication with the divine is a central feature in nearly all religious or spiritual participation. Prayer and/or meditation can be practiced as corporate or individual, spoken, silent, in movement, with use of language, or without linguistic structure. Active participation in the practice of prayer is not a matter of outward or visible indicators but rather is a state of being in open attunement. Being in a state of open attunement (via prayer, meditation, or mindfulness) correlates with areas of the brain that orient us in the world and with alpha brain waves.[7] During these practices, our brain's orientation

7. Newberg and D'Aquili, *Why God Won't Go Away.*

area decreases in activity facilitating a felt experience of connecting with a presence larger and more expansive than ourselves at the same time that we are in state of relaxed focus that keeps us engaged in the experience. The experience of engaged, relaxed connection is an important counter balance to the experience of disengaged, numbed, disconnection that is experienced in traumatic dissociation and depression that correlates with theta brain waves. Engaged participation in prayer, meditation, or mindfulness has the potential to function as a form of neurofeedback training in that it builds safe familiarity with the experience of alpha wave alterations of orientation as different from the theta wave alterations of orientation present as a part of trauma survival and response. A note of attention and care: due to the close proximity of alpha and theta waves in their frequency, it is important to hone awareness of and attunement to the felt sense of active engagement verses dissociative disengagement in order for the practice of prayer or meditation to be restorative rather than reinforcing of trauma response. The tendency to slide into dissociative disengagement (which can often initiate flashbacks) may be one of the reasons why survivors of trauma might discontinue their practices of prayer while in the midst of traumatic response and processing. Simply offering the invitation for congregants to "soften your gaze" or "direct your intention towards God" rather than "close your eyes" during corporate prayer is a helpful step in generating greater safety. Nevertheless, relaxed engagement during the spiritual discipline of prayer and meditation open up opportunities to reinforce neurological pathways of resiliency as well as provide an attuned connection to the grounded, centered, compassionate, curious, courageous Self within each of us. Growing a felt awareness of Self allows us to be more clearly aware of the wounded and burdened parts within us and others. The spiritual disciplines and practices of prayer and meditation, in our corporate and communal prayers, individual supplications, moving mindfulness in yoga, Tai Chi, or labyrinth walking, still contemplation, and all other manifestations, have the capacity to facilitate resiliency through experiences of open connection with the divine presence. Additionally, when prayer or meditation is experienced in a communal setting that includes moving, speaking, or chanting with others, it also enhances our capacity for being in rhythm with others.

The greatest repository of resources and strength communities of faith hold as distinct from other communities in society are the rituals that mark many of the most important milestones in our lives. The importance of ritual participation is difficult to overstate as evidenced in the presence of rituals across all human cultures and epochs. At their most basic formulation, rituals establish the rhythms of life in community while also marking significant life transitions—from childhood into adulthood, from singleness to relational commitment, from separateness to inclusion, and from life into death. Through embodied participation, rituals connect us as individuals with the larger narrative of community, world, and the divine. They provide a structured, somatic, narrated, multi-sensory, rhythmic path as we journey through a full emotional range of life experience. From the joy of creation and union to the chaos of injury, through the pain and sorrow of grief and loss to the gratitude and appreciation of life, our rituals provide a template to continue moving through the joys and struggles of our lives. A point for creative imagination is to explore how and in what ways the journey of trauma exposure, response, processing, and resiliency can find space and honor within our ritual structures. Would this simply require an opening up of awareness to the trauma already voiced in our rituals surrounding crucifixion and resurrection, or those of creation, violation, and desire for restoration? Or do we need new rituals to midwife us through the process of trauma recovery?

The practices cultivated over thousands of years of spiritual seeking, connection, and meaning making are rich resources for the care of souls, minds, and bodies. The question is not whether our religious traditions have a wealth of wisdom and care to offer in the face of traumatic injury and wounding; rather, it is how to bring informed awareness to our growing understanding of the prevalence and impact of trauma into the crafting of our regular communal gatherings and individual spiritual disciplines. Religious communities have long been the bastions of hope, meaning, and connection in times of grief and despair as well as sources of shared joy and resiliency. Opening up these gifts to the potential of caring for the wounds of traumatic overwhelm and violation requires only a shift in intention. Yet, this shift in intention and attention does require courage to acknowledge the depth of trauma in our lives and society and a boldness to speak the truth when it is easier to remain silent or unaware. While there may be a felt sense of risk with regard to how acknowledgement of trauma will be received by our communities, we must remember that many of those for whom we care are already living in the valley of the shadow of trauma. They already know of the impact of traumatic wounding in their own lives and the lives of loved ones. When we can speak about the truth of trauma, we begin a process that can depathologize traumatic response as a shame increasing sign of moral and spiritual failure and honor the courage of survival in the face of the original traumatic wounding and the fight to continue through traumatic response. Taking on the honorable responsibility of offering survivors the primary care of ritual participation that connects one to one's Self, community, and the divine may also open up spaces to consider our God language and imagery differently. As human beings continue to live in community, learn about our world, face new challenges, and strive to life with love and authenticity, our religious confessions and spiritual journeys must continue to evolve. The language and imagery of past eras authentically encapsulated their understanding and experience in the world and with the divine. While some of these images hold significance and resonance through a multitude of eras, there is also wisdom in the courageous and faithful willingness to continue to explore other images, concepts, and the lenses of interpretation to resonate with our current world experience.

4

Communicating and Interpreting Trauma

Trauma-sensitive theology and praxis requires seeing traumatic wounding, naming it as trauma and understanding the ways in which traumatic wounding impacts various systems of the survivor and community, and cultivating practices that can support resiliency and recovery from traumatic overwhelm and injury. Identifying, rightly naming, and honoring the struggle of traumatic experience and response are vital steps in responding to and accompanying survivors on the journey towards resiliency. However, as care providers, it is not enough to see, name, and accompany; we also must attend to how traumatic experience is interpreted and communicated within our communities and in our society. Those of us not actively struggling with post traumatic response have a responsibility to communicate the struggles of living with post traumatic responses while also offering the hope of resiliency. This requires a delicate balance and an intentional awareness of various forms of social privilege, use of hermeneutical lenses through which to view trauma, and a willingness to acknowledge narratives of trauma in our religious texts and traditions. This chapter focuses on these three areas of privilege, hermeneutics, and text.

COMMUNICATING TRAUMA
AND COMMUNAL LEADERSHIP

Community, communion, communication . . . three words that are integral to leadership of and within communities of Christian faith. All three are rooted in the notion of commune, "to converse or talk together, usually with profound intensity, intimacy, etc.; interchange thoughts or feelings or to be in intimate communication or rapport."[1] Communing with one another and/or God, sharing a deep intimacy and connection requires faith in the health of relationality and a courageous vulnerability to share the depths of who one is with another. It also requires a foundation of trust and right relationship. For those who have experienced traumatic wounding, faith and trust in the healthy boundaries of right relationship can be a challenge. For many, the very cause of traumatic wounding is the betrayal of relational trust and safety. Nevertheless, one of the fundamental components of fostering resiliency is healthy community support and safe relationships with others and with self. Renewing faith in communal safety and support with the accompanying restoration of the hope in the reliability of the first line of defense in a crisis, social engagement is one of the areas in which religious communities can make a profound impact in fostering resiliency from traumatic wounding. Communities of faith already have well established rituals and practices that can offer safety and connection when offered with compassionate awareness, intention, and informed communication.

Communication between persons or between an individual and their environment is comprised, in its most basic articulation, of a stimulus, reception of information, and interpretation of the stimulus. With regard to navigating our environment, stimuli is offered by our environment, received via our sense organs, and interpreted based on previously established schemas that are both contextual and socially informed. Our brains have two pathways that are utilized in receiving sensory stimulation. In the first pathway, sensory information is received by our limbic system and, if there is any risk of threat, our body moves directly into protective maneuvers of social engagement, fight/flight, or freeze. The second pathway also begins in the limbic system but then includes a process of discernment or interpretation in the frontal cortex before engaging in action. The first process is faster but less accurate; the second is slower but more accurate. The clearest experience of this two pronged system in my life was when I was running by myself on a natural trail one spring. I was lost in my thoughts and turned a corner in the trail and saw a long, serpentine shape on the trail. Having been on the receiving end of a rattlesnake rattle warning in my childhood and with no option for social engagement, my body system immediately interpreted the shape as a snake, ramped up my threat response system, and shifted into a sprint. A few seconds later, once I was at a safe

1. Dictionary.com, "Commune."

enough distance, my brains interpretative system kicked in, I stopped my sprint, and turned back to see that the serpentine shape was not a serpent but was just a tree branch. I took a deep breath, activating my parasympathetic nervous system, shook my head feeling a bit silly at my overreaction, and went about my run. The learning that often results from experiences of crisis events or traumatic wounding has the potential to amplify the brain's use of the first pathway of receiving and responding to sensory stimuli and correspond to the clinical symptoms of hypervigilance and an increased startle response.

For communities of faith who desire to support recovery from traumatic wounding in individuals or their community, understanding the process of how our brains/bodies receive and process information can illuminate means of compassion and intervention. Communing with our external environments includes communing with our own perceptions, prior learnings, and physiological responses as we hope to move from reaction to interpretation to interrelational communication. Going back to my run in the woods, once the immediate experience has passed questions remain: How do I understand my experience? How would I share may experience with others? To what degree do I anticipate that others would share a similar enough experience that I feel confident in being understood? Will someone else "get it"? What form of care would I hope or need to receive? How do I commune with others to share information and receive mirroring of my experience? Sharing personal experiences with others via verbal or written communication always entails the possibility of misunderstanding due to the great variety of human experience and response. Communication of care or communication about one's own experience of traumatic wounding is more tenuous than communication about other subjects due to the presence of traumatic overwhelm.

Communicating the reality of traumatic exposure, response, and recovery with honesty, compassion, and courage means holding together the experience of wounding and hope for healing. All communication requires a spiral movement of the intention of the speaker, the means of communication, reception of the means of communication, interpretation of the message by the listener, and response by the listener.[2] For communication to be effective and facilitate healthy relationality, these five movements should be fluid and constant. When there is a misalignment between any adjoining steps, the communication is bound to be ineffective or potentially harmful.

---

2. Baldwin, "Akroatic Embodied Hearing," 73–88.

With regard to constructing a trauma-sensitive theology and practice, this spiral movement of communication and care requires an informed, clear, and compassionate intention, verbal, kinesthetic, energetic, or written communication, reception of narrative and somatic presence with tenderness and belief, interpretation of communication embracing alterity, multiplicity, empathy, and accountability, and response emerging from a desire for full and multi-dimensional recovery.

Experiences of traumatic wounding extend beyond the initial injury. On the individual scale, the impact of trauma can profoundly influence many of the areas of life discussed in the chapter 2. On the social scale, acts of violence and violation threaten who we are as a community and society. Just as the model of Internal Family Systems is helpful for illuminating an individual's internal psychological landscape, it is also helpful for revealing the ways in which a community or society responds to trauma. In moments of societal trauma, parts of the population retreat into hiding out of fear of retaliatory violence or deny the impact of violence, parts lash out seeking vengeance and retribution, and other parts work to fix, manage, control, or negotiate a "measured response." And just like the parts of our internal personal system, the various parts of society have good intentions but generally unsustainable or destructive strategies. Cultivating Self-energy and leadership on a communal level is a significant challenge and requires community leadership that already demonstrates the qualities of Self and has sufficient trust established with and among individual community members. Community leadership may be embodied by the person formally leading the group or it could emerge from within the group. Some persons who are designated as the leader may readily slip into the role of a manager rather than function to ground and center the community with clarity, compassion, curiosity, courage, and calmness. Understanding and interpreting the impact of traumatic experiences requires a grounded, centered, compassionate presence that leads from a place of care and openness.

For those of us honored with the responsibility of community leadership and care for survivors of trauma (either traumatized parts of our self or others), the way we talk about traumatic events and post traumatic response is important. When community leaders speak with informed compassion and resist the temptation of pathologizing survivors, we open or expand avenues of resiliency and recovery. Resisting the pull of pathologizing doesn't mean that we minimize the impact of harm of traumatic wounds. It does mean that we maintain hope in the resiliency of survivors

and the innate resources we are blessed with to restore balance. Communication that opens avenues of care includes all areas of congregational life
and leadership including homiletics, liturgy, adult education, and pastoral
care. Simply naming the reality of traumatic wounding in our culture and
lives with compassion and tenderness begins to establish safety that can
counter shame and grow into resiliency.

PRIVILEGE OF NON-PRIMARY TRAUMATIZATION

One common mistake made when offering care to a group of persons with
chronic suffering is the privileging of one's own experience over the experience of the one who suffers. The social frames of racial, gender, sexual orientation, and class privilege are well established at this point in contemporary
Christian theology and care. Social privilege is, for simplicity sake, getting
to not have to worry about things in order to safely navigate life. I experience my white privilege when I do not worry about being shot by a police
officer if pulled over in my car (though I do worry about the possibility of
being groped). My education grants me social privilege in that I have access
to resources of learning and social influence. My cis-gender presentation
and sexual orientation that currently conforms to heterosexual norms allows me to hold my partner's hand or offer a short kiss in public without
fear of violence or threat. These areas of social privilege allow me to occupy
spaces in the world with less fear and legitimate concern for violence than
persons who are black, Latino/a, Asian, less educated, trans-, gay or lesbian.
On the other side, my embodiment as female increases my social vulnerability in terms of pay for work, experience of actual and threatened assault,
and less representation in houses of institutional power. I worry more about
my physical safety than the men in my life do. Likewise, as a trauma survivor, I am more vulnerable to secondary assault than others, have (at times)
struggled to complete the tasks of my education and profession due to post
traumatic responses, fear judgment and decreased chance of employment
if my experience/s of violation are discovered, and having my concerns and
insights discounted as reflective of "being a victim" (though this is not an
identity marker I have ever utilized for myself). For those who have experienced chronic traumatization, the impact of post traumatic response creeps
into many areas of life and functions as a pervasive form of oppression.

Recognizing the "privilege of non-traumatization" (wherein traumatic response meets the intensity and criteria of clinical presentation

of posttraumatic stress) is an essential lens for those writing about or researching trauma and for those providing a vast array of care for people and communities who experience traumatic wounding. When scholars, clinicians, and clergy fail to adequately recognize and own their position with respect to the privilege of non-traumatization, we inevitably contribute to additional harm. For scholars, this shows up when traumatology researchers pathologize survival responses and end up treating survivors as broken, defective, or risky. It is revealed in literature that discusses survivors as "they," a group that clearly doesn't include the author and is painted as "other" in an invalidating manner. For clinicians, this privilege presents in an increased fear of risk in conflating and naming trauma survivors as "borderlines" or in failing to also hold onto the resources of resiliency while caring for the depths of traumatic wounding. For clergy, the privilege of non-traumatization is revealed in an absence of care and attention and in holding an assumption that "these things don't happen in my congregation."

The privilege of non-traumatization facilitates a blindness to the reality of traumatic wounding that buffers the person with privilege from those who are wounded. Like other forms of social privilege, the privilege of non-traumatization allows the one/s holding privilege to live without added considerations for safety and survival or to allocate resources (financial, energetic, and social) for generativity or pleasure rather than survival or recovery—therapy to support traumatic processing and resiliency is expensive and requires significant time and effort. The ability to allocate resources into areas of life other than survival and recovery is privilege. The ability to live out from underneath the shadow of post traumatic response and impact is privilege. This privilege, like all other forms, creates a separation in our social relationships unless we acknowledge our privilege with humility and a desire to hear and amplify the voices of those who don't experience the benefits of "getting to not pay attention."

Rebalancing the privilege of non-traumatization requires knowledge, care, humility, and compassion. The four primary commitments of trauma-sensitive theology and practice—the priority of bodily experience, full acceptance of trauma narratives, natural given-ness of human psychological multiplicity, and faith in the robust resiliency of trauma survivors—facilitate the movement of recognition of the privilege of non-traumatization and building of practices of care by attending to key areas of our theological lives and articulations that have rendered traumatic wounding nearly invisible. The first step is seeing what is invisible and then understanding the impact of the wounding. After making visible the invisible, we must take on the task of compassionate interpretation, the task of hermeneutics. Trauma informed and trauma-sensitive hermeneutics is important in providing a protective buffer against additional traumatization of the survivor of traumatic wounding and protects those with the privilege of non-traumatization from unwitting arrogance or unintentionally perpetrating additional harm or shame.

TRAUMA SENSITIVE HERMENEUTICS

In its most basic articulation, hermeneutics is the process and set of lenses one uses to interpret "texts." Texts are most commonly associated with written documents or sacred manuscripts but can also be expanded to include any medium of communication including visual art, music, dance, or body posture. For the construction of a trauma-sensitive theology and practice, trauma-sensitive hermeneutics receives as subject or "text" the embodied narratives of survivors of traumatic wounding as witnessed in our sacred texts and in the persons in our midst. Like a pair of glasses or contacts that allow a person with impaired vision to see more clearly, the lenses offered in the practice of trauma-sensitive hermeneutics seek to clarify and illuminate. The four lenses of trauma-sensitive hermeneutics are: the hermeneutics of alterity, multiplicity, empathy, and accountability. These lenses build on one another and provide a framework for interpreting narratives of traumatic wounding that contribute to compassion and resiliency.

In her opening remarks on the role of hermeneutics for religion and science discourse, Archbishop Antje Jackelén states, "Hermeneutics is what turns suspicion from a vice into an art."[3] Suspicion as vice fuels re-traumatization and pathologizes survivors of traumatic wounding thus adding burden and insult to injury. Suspicion as art is simply grounded and compassionate curiosity. The hermeneutical lenses of trauma-sensitive theology receive their guidance from a clear understanding of traumatic wounding and processing with the intention of honoring difference, embracing all parts of self, offering empathy and companionship, and requiring justice and accountability. Correspondingly, I would offer that hermeneutics is what turns suspicion into compassion. Let us now turn attention to each of our hermeneutic lenses one at a time.

---

3. Jackelén, *Dialogue.*

Hermeneutics of Alterity

Compassion is the energy that links each of us together in recognition of a shared humanity or a shared life (with regard to non-human species). The strands that draw us together facilitate healthy attachments and secure affection. The beauty of compassionate togetherness, perhaps counter intuitively, requires a recognition of separation or difference. This separation and recognition of difference is not an intention to harm or to exile; but an intention to truly see another as a being deserving of honor and autonomy. One of the ways that I more fully witness my individuality and unique personal characteristics is to be in relationship with others who are individually or culturally different than I am. Frequently, it is only through encountering another that we more fully recognize our self. For instance, I grew up in the South, a region steeped in Baptist communities of faith, and attended a Baptist church as an adolescent and a University that is historically affiliated with the Baptist religious tradition. However, it was not being in the midst of sea of Baptists that lead me to realize how much Baptist polity and diversity of theology seeped into by being; rather, it was moving to the Midwest and living and learning amongst Lutherans. Only when coming into close contact with Protestant Christians who lived out their polity and theology differently than my own faith communities of origin did I really become aware of the distinctive characteristics that define Baptist faith and life. I was more specifically Baptist in the midst of Lutherans than I ever was among fellow Baptists. Encounters with those whose practices and formative lenses differ from our own is a rich gift in deepening our own self awareness and identity. Alterity is ultimately not a threat but a gift. Cultivating personal identity and an awareness of personal identity facilitates the development of healthy, properly balanced attachments with others. Recognition of self is required for true recognition of another; and, recognition of the other (whether an external person or internal part) is required for full recognition of Self.

Trauma sensitive hermeneutics begins with the lens of alterity. Alterity is fundamentally a recognition of "the other" or "otherness." Otherness corresponds to an acknowledgment of the difference among persons and the diversity within the human and ecological community. It recognizes that I am different and distinct from you. Our lived experiences vary and the context from which we emerge and the context we now live in are different from one another. Recognition of alterity is the first step in the healthy separation and establishment of boundaries that ultimately allows us to cultivate relationships. Recognition of alterity begins with somatic attunement to our own bodies and the connections among proprioceptive sensation, affect, and parts of oneself. When we are able to notice, honor, and attend to the tensions of desires, obligations, or needs as expressed in our somatic sensations, emotions, and social roles, we grow and deepen our ability to welcome intra- (or internal) and interrelationality.

A hermeneutic of alterity is an essential lens for the construction of trauma-sensitive theology and practice because it sets the conditions for our capacity to fully attend to the multiplicity within society and within our self, the cultivation of empathy, and bolstering of accountability. Borrowing again from the insights of Internal Family Systems, internal psychological harmony requires that all parts are welcome and receive care. When we are unable to recognize our hurting or overwhelmed parts or when our system exiles or banishes those parts, they show up in unhealthy patterns of behavior and reactions. To reference and riff on the Early Church Father, Gregory of Nazianzus, that which is not assumed, or welcomed, cannot be healed or redeemed.

The hermeneutic of alterity allows us to glimpse the other in our midst and in our own being and offers us the opportunity to either welcome or to exile. When we choose to welcome, we open up possibilities for compassionate understanding and healing resolution. When we choose to exile, we increase the felt sense of isolation, abandonment, and accompanying pain and distrust. The lens of alterity is essential in cultivating awareness of the other in our midst and in our self so that we have the capacity to choose our response. Choice, in this matter, is the beginning of claiming agency and appropriate and healthy uses of relational power. In contemporary discourse, there is a fine line and balancing act of acknowledging "the other" without "otherizing." When we receive the presence of the other with fear, judgment, or condemnation, we make the other an object thereby diminishing the humanity of the person before us as well as our own humanity. When we receive the presence of the other (internally or externally) with compassion, curiosity, courage, and clarity, we see the other as benefit to our collective wellbeing—even if the other is currently disruptive or utilizing unhelpful strategies in an effort to establish safety.

The beautiful and challenging variations of human experience are whitewashed when a drive toward universal and unitary expression trumps the multitude of diverse, intersectional, and contextual realities. Attention to the great variety of experience necessitates an honoring of the "other-ness" in self and in relationship. Recognition of alterity is not merely a philosophical trope. It is imperative in creating just societies and communities and is rooted in an awareness of the alterity within each individual.

Hermeneutics of Multiplicity

Once we more fully witness the alterity that is present in society and in our communities, we begin to develop an understanding of the vast variety of human be-ing, experience, and context. Each of us emerges from our own matrix of experiences in the world and in relationships—we are each a unique product of our unique context. As we attend more care-fully and attentively to the diversity around us, we also begin to recognize the diversity within us. A quick internal survey of the variety of desires, conflicts, intentions, or skills that make up who we are as individuals illuminates the multiplicity of parts within each of us. These parts are recognized by attending to the great variety of thoughts, sensations, emotions, and roles that constitute our daily lives. Walt Whitman's well known poem "Song of Myself" includes the lines "Do I contradict myself? / Very well then I contradict myself, / (I am large, I contain multitudes.)"[4] Whitman poetically highlights the natural human internal multiplicity that emerges from healthy psychological development.

The internal multiplicity that undergirds each of us permits us to adapt to a variety of relational and environment encounters. Recognition and honoring of the alterity within is the foundation of healthy recognition of alterity in others and is a precondition for a hermeneutic of multiplicity that takes seriously the presence and perspective of otherness that is highlighted through alterity. Multiplicity as a hermeneutical lens is essential for the construction of trauma-sensitive theological thinking and religious practice. It is essential because it provides a window for interpreting our own great variety of responses and intentions as well as acknowledging the great variety present in others. Theologically, a hermeneutics of multiplicity opens up avenues of creative theological construction that honors the wisdoms of our denominational and religious traditions while also providing a non-threatening means for authentic encounters with traditions and wisdoms that are outside our inherited systems. The gains in wisdom and creativity that emerge through authentic engagement with difference

4. Whitman, *Leaves of Grass*.

and multiplicity can function as the components of necessary and healthy theological re/formation.

A hermeneutics of multiplicity is not only vitally important for intra- and inter-personal encounters; it is of great import for theological reflection and faithful confession of the divine and provides a novel lens as an alternative to theologies that corral power into systems of hierarchy. When systems of power fail to attend to alterity and multiplicity, they are at an increased risk of abusing relational power in a manner that increases traumatic wounding. Traumatic wounding occurs when we fail to see the multiplicity of practices and doctrines within religious traditions, racial groups, and/or nationalities in addition to the great variety of ways in which human being identify groups of living organisms. Honoring the multiplicity in creation, humanity, and individual persons is requisite for fostering recovery and resiliency from traumatic wounding. When I can learn to care for the exiled and traumatized parts of my self in addition to the vast array of pro-social and/or destructive protective parts, I can begin to recognize and offer care to those in the larger community who are exiled/traumatized, controlling, and/or impulsively destructive. The ability to offer compassionate care for one's own internal system of multiplicity constructs a bridge of empathy to offer care to others.

Hermeneutics of Empathy

In the construction of a trauma-sensitive theology, the hermeneutical lens of empathy facilitates our capacity to recognize connection and care. Empathy is the basis of all appropriate responses to survivors of traumatic experiences and begins with an assumption of shared, yet distinctly individualized, human affective response and meaning making. While each person has their own distinct history of interpersonal interactions, learned schema for ordering new experiences, and internal narratives, empathy is what allows us to put ourselves "in another person's shoes" with the intention of compassionate understanding rather than "fixing." The compassionate and curious opening of interpretation then becomes the source of a hermeneutic of empathy. If hermeneutics provides the lens or fore-structure through which we interpret and understand, then a hermeneutic of empathy is what allows us to avoid inflicting further traumatization on the survivor/s of traumatic wounding.

Empathy, as distinct from sympathy as a "feeling with," centers on a "feeling or sensing into" the experience of another. While sympathy includes a joining with the other in a more complete way than empathy, the recognition of the experience of the other while retaining one's own experience is the strength of empathetic response. It is akin to saying that one has aware compassion for the struggle while still retaining enough self distinction to provide balanced assistance. Empathy begins with a pause in order to receive information as communicated by another without superimposing our experience or interpretation on top of the one who is sharing. It seeks to understand with as much clarity as possible what the experience what like for the survivor and then to join alongside the survivor as a supportive partner rather than authority. Empathy is an innate human capacity, a skill that requires fostering and honing, and a resource for connection and care.

This form of interpretative care requires a balance of connection and honoring of difference. In a ministry of pastoral care, if the care giver becomes fully involved in the emotional content of the care receiver, then the care giver can no longer offer the kind of stable care that is required by the care receiver. The balance point between feeling into while remaining distinct is a challenge for many individuals; however, the challenge is more easily met with an honoring of alterity and an awareness of multiplicity. A hermeneutic of empathy offers the lenses of understanding, contextualization, and compassion in the process of understanding and interpreting traumatic wounding and resiliency.

Hermeneutics of Accountability

The fourth lens for constructing trauma-sensitive theology is the hermeneutic of accountability. The intention of this lens is to bring into focus narratives of traumatic wounding and facilitate the naming of those narratives as trauma. Too often, experiences of trauma and traumatic wounding get named as something other than trauma. Historically this mis-nomenclature has been a combination of an unspoken, yet powerful, cultural mandate to disassociate from traumatic witness and naming and a nascent and undeveloped understanding of the prevalence and impact of traumatic wounding. For instance, Freud's early work with women who had experienced the trauma of incest shifted in focus from traumatic wounding to a notion of fantasy and desire. The prevailing diagnosis of hysteria both blinded people from seeing the reality of traumatic violations of boundaries and contributed to therapies that amplified post traumatic response. During World War I, post traumatic response was named as "shell shock" and was thought to indicate a weakness in character or morality on the part of the soldier. Currently, we regularly mistake the ways individuals and communities attempt to survive institutional and intergenerational trauma as indicators of lack of moral fiber or ambition to make their lives better. These misnamings obscure the reality of traumatic wounding under interpretations that blame the injured party for the wound. When we fail to provide an informed and honest accounting of the prevalence of traumatic injury by choosing instead to mis-represent traumatic violation and injury, we compound the burden carried by survivors. Accountability requires courageous witness, correct naming, accurate accounting, and robust justice in holding the perpetrators of relational violence accountable for their actions.

TRAUMA IN OUR TEXTS

The discipline of hermeneutics originated as a means of interpreting sacred texts and bridging the differences between the culture at the time of authorship and the culture of the reader. The hermeneutical lenses of alterity, multiplicity, empathy, and accountability that are formative for constructing trauma-sensitive theology and practices also seek to illuminate the context of the text as distinct from that of contemporary readers, honor the multiple voices and intentions of sacred texts, cultivate empathy between persons in the narratives, the reader, and persons in our lives, and to provide an accounting of the presence of traumatic narratives within the text. The interpretative process can progress in both directions—from alterity to accountability and from accountability to alterity. For some the necessary first step is to see the narratives of trauma within the text and to name them as trauma. Once we can take account of the narratives of trauma in the text, we can bridge the space between reader and text via empathy, noticing our own multiple responses and the multiplicity of responses in our communities of faith, and then seeing more clearly the alterity within and among us. The journey of trauma-sensitive hermeneutics has many entry points and connections that all ultimately facilitate more accurate interpretation and acknowledgment of trauma in our texts. Traumatic experiences have occurred throughout human history as testified to throughout Christian scripture, including the ostracism of the first people from the garden, the murder of Able by Cain, the fall of the tower of Babel and consequent rendering of human community, the rape of Tamar, the slavery and oppression of the Hebrews by Egyptians, exile of the people of Israel during the Assyrian and Babylonian takeovers, unexpected pregnancy of Mary which threatened her social ability to survive, the mental illness of the man possessed by Legion, the crucifixion of Jesus, and the exile of John of Patmos, just to name a few prominent examples. However, despite the rampant violence and trauma in the text, most theologians have either neglected to name these events as traumatic or have sought to sacralize violence and trauma up to the point of being nearly salvific (e.g., instructions for individuals to model the self-sacrifice of Jesus).

Religious texts are at their most basic function stories told and retold with the intention of providing structure and meaning for life in community. They are stories of people of faith daring to live in relationship with the divine, whether named as God, YHWH, Allah, Buddah, Gaia, Shiva, etc., and in the world, community, and relationships. They are stories of hope, violence, promise, passion, despair, confusion, pain, and love. Sacred narratives captivate us when they meaningfully reflect the deep, existential questions, pains, and concerns that are shared among humanity. Who am I? Is there something bigger than what I see that guides life and history? Am I loved? Do I matter? How do we survive in the midst of oppression or exile? How do I make sense of my experiences in the world? Am I safe enough? What is my role or my purpose? Most theological scholars across religious traditions will argue that the power of sacred texts is their capacity to mirror back to us the great diversity of lived experience and help us make meaning out of our experiences. The alterity within the Christian scriptures not only reflects various intentions, purposes, and communities of authorship; they also reflect a great diversity of lived experience with regard to class, education, oppression, attachment, and traumas (primary, secondary, intergenerational, societal, and cultural).

Sacred texts, as narratives of humanity's endeavor to live faithfully with God and amongst creation, include lamentation and trauma in addition to joy and healing. It is the range of emotional connection and honesty found within the texts that facilitate their power and resonante with readers and persons of faith. If these texts only presented stories of utopian life, they would have ended in the creation narratives of Genesis chapters one and two. It is the honest inclusion of the ways in which human beings inflict and experience violence at the hands of one another that contributes to the importance of these texts. When we try to hide, exile, or explain away the violence in our text, we also end up hiding, exiling, or explaining away the violence in our society. Recognizing the violence and sin in our sacred narratives is not a way to justify or valorize violence; it is an accounting that should hold us accountable to our actions that are destructive uses of power. The hermeneutic of multiplicity allows us to see the ways in which we contribute to overt and covert systems of violence at the same time in which we honor the ways in which we have been victims of violence. The multiplicity of voices and uses of power in the text reflect the multiplicity of the variety of voices and uses of power in our communities, relationships, and even within our own being.

Sacred texts emerge from the cultures and cultural norms of their authorship. In this sense, they are a window into the past. They reveal something about humanity, knowledge, and the dynamics of communal and national life in their era. A hermeneutics of empathy allows us, the contemporary reader, to connect with the dimensions of shared life between ourselves and the persons in the text. If we allow ourselves, we can feel into the affective experiences of people whose lives are very different than our own but with whom we share the common struggles of life, love, hope, faith, oppression, and survival. Empathic connection with the persons in our texts can provide a buffer against the feelings of hopelessness, isolation, despair, fear, and/or helplessness that can overwhelm in times of primary, secondary, or societal trauma. For instance, I was a senior in college on September 11, 2001 and at that point in my life had read the Bible cover to cover three times and the entirely of the Christian Testament easily over a dozen. I recall gathering in my college's convocation center that afternoon for a university gathering and prayer/worship service. The dean of chapel and one of my academic advisors, Dr. Richard Wilson, preached that afternoon on the falling of the tower of Siloam from the Gospel of Luke. The narrative of the tower falling is only mentioned as an aside in a single verse and almost always glossed over in this passage that is predominantly about sin and repentance; however, on that day, the narrative about a tower falling and killing innocent people resonated powerfully. A hermeneutic of empathy over judgment provided a space for grief, confusion, fear that could be honored and held rather than becoming a rationale for hasty vindication and further violence. Offering a connection of empathy between the present and narrative past functioned, in those moments, as a holding place to honor all the emotions and parts that were activated by violence and facilitate a more grounded and clear response. Sacred texts have the capacity to hold the depth and breadth of human emotion and experience and provide a lens for right response, not as a literal blueprint of how to order society but as a repository of a great variety of human experience and affect, when interpreted with care and wisdom.

When engaging in systemic or constructive theology or homiletics, how one utilizes and interprets sacred texts matters. What role and with what weight do sacred texts hold in our articulation of the faith? Are sacred texts interpreted literally, figuratively, holistically, individually, etc.? Which is privileged: the cultural context of the author or the reader? Theological reflection on sacred texts requires interpretative choices that will directly influence how our faith is embodied and lived out in private and public spheres. As I tell my students, "the God you preach and believe, is the society you get." When our interpretation of sacred texts generates a theology that deifies power and empire, we get a society that values power and empire above all else. When our interpretation of sacred texts generates a theology that values care for the suffering and justice, we get a society that cares for the vulnerable and seeks justice. Trauma-sensitive theology seeks to highlight within sacred texts narratives that honor the harm of traumatic wounding and facilitate healing resiliency. The hope is that honest acknowledgement of the presence of traumatic experiences and wounding within our sacred texts can open up narratives of resonance to facilitate resiliency.

PART TWO

Constructing Trauma-Sensitive Theology

5

Pre-Traumatic Creation

AT THE BEGINNING . . .

It is customary at the beginning of a journey on the path of systematic theology to include a prolegomena—an articulation of the methods, frameworks, or guiding commitments. As we set off on our venture of constructing a systematic trauma-sensitive theology, there are a few remarks that feel important to state with clarity and directness.

First, I firmly and with conviction believe that theology matters! How human beings, as individuals, communities, societies, and as a species, think about and articulate our understanding of God or the divine is consequential in how we relate to others, our world, and our self. Theology is not just the purview of some academics in a classroom; it is a foundational activity of all of us—whether or not we directly recognize or acknowledge our personal theologies. The ways in which we make sense of our lived existence in relation to others is an outflow of how we understand and enact power, relationality, agency, and responsibility. Theological systems that prioritize static, unchanging, transcendent forms of power are likely to find expression in social systems that value sameness, conventionality, and deferment to persons who possess power. Theological systems that prioritize dynamics, variability, imminence, and intimate care for life are likely to find expression in social systems that value diversity, variety, innovation, and voices of dissent to agents of power. How we preach about God and the divine's relationship with the world, society, and individuals does find expression in the ways in which people live in the world. Theology matters!

Second, because theology matters, it is important to embrace the wisdom of the Reformers that theological confessions remain open to additional re/formation. Theology, like many other disciplines and practices, is a reflection of how human beings understand the world. Theology is the task of interpretation and meaning making and draws on a variety of sources including holy texts, traditions of thought and practice, contemporary multidisciplinary knowledge, and lived experience. Just as our understanding of global geography shifted from a flat Earth to a spherical Earth and most of us generally don't consider the gesture of saying "Bless you" after a sneeze a necessary mini exorcism to keep the evil spirit causing a cold from re-entering the person, it is essential for our theology to continue to grow and remain connected and relevant to our understanding of the world. For the construction of a Trauma-Sensitive Theology, the capacity and willingness to adjust our theological confessions permits religious followers, leaders, and spiritual care professionals to see traumatic response as a natural human process of resiliency that has become stuck rather than a sign of demon possession or lack of faith. Karl Barth, a pillar of twentieth-century theology, is credited as saying something akin to "we need to preach or read with the Bible in one hand, and a newspaper in the other" and, in our current era, events that evoke trauma are on the front page nearly every day. Theological engagement cannot afford to remain detached from understanding events in the world if it is to remain relevant and a resource for faithful living. It must honor the wise tradition of scholarship and faithful witness that came before and have the courage to be reformed to meet the great needs of each age.

Third, in my theological development I have had the fortuitous opportunity to learn amongst scholars from a variety of Protestant Christian theological traditions and was formed within a tradition that historically valued theological diversity within the community over strict adherence to one way of thinking or worshipping. As a consequence, I realize that I have cultivated a theological position that welcomes wisdom and insights from a great variety faithful thinkers. Trauma-Sensitive Theology, as I offer here, is not intended to be a definitive formulation; rather, it is one way of thinking through a variety of commitments and remains open. The intention is not to generate a set of positions to establish an/other "orthodoxy." It is to begin, or continue, to imagine how a shift in one area of theological confession reverberates in and through other areas. It is a process of creative engagement seeking to honor the mystery of the divine energy or presence which finds expression in the Christian God and Jesus, the Israelite YWHW, the Hindu deities, etc. while also holding on to the humility of knowing that we don't know it all and all theological articulations are incomplete.

Finally, why a systematic theology? "Systematic theology," which found its heyday in the latter 19th and first half of the 20th century, has fallen out of fashion for contemporary theology which tends to prefer "contextual theology." The shift in language and intent is a move from the Modern and Enlightenment predispositions towards ordered hierarchies of life and an aim for a "universal" knowledge to the more weblike relationality of postmodernism and honest clarity that "human experience" is widely diverse and cannot be whitewashed into a single perspective. While I clearly affirm the importance of relationality and honoring the specific and varied contexts from which we emerge, I also find the connections among theological loci, assumed in the framework of systematic theology, exceedingly helpful. Each dimension of our faith is connected to, influences, and is influenced by the other dimensions of theological confession. The exquisite relational connections among points that are directly addressed in systematic theologies do not have to be considered linearly or hierarchically; they can, with equal authenticity, be imaged as a highly connected web or matrix. Seen through relational lenses, the move away from systematics becomes unnecessary and a path opens to reclaim focused attention on the relationship of doctrinal formation with awareness and care towards the multiplicity of human experience and context. Trauma-Sensitive Theology is an attempt at a systematic, contextual theology. It is systematic in its attention to traditional theological loci and how shifts in one impact the others. It is contextual in its primary care towards lived experiences of traumatic wounding, post traumatic response, and resiliency. It is not an attempt towards a "universal" theology that resonates with all human contexts. It is a creative, faith/ful exploration into how theology can function to validate the wounding of traumatic overwhelm and take care to avoid retraumatizing survivors or engage in practices that are theologically or spiritually abusive.

"To be a theologian is to be on the boundary."[1] David Blumenthal's conceptualization of the place of the theologian on the boundary with multiple responsibilities "to be a voice for the tradition, speak for God, defend God, speak for one's fellow human beings, be in solidarity with one's fellow human beings before God, speak the 'ought', and have prior commitments"

---

1. Blumenthal, *Facing the Abusing God*, 3.

has longed shaped my understanding of the role of the theologian in the life of faith and the world.[2] I most appreciate the honest, authenticity of his vision of the theologian in both making bold claims for and about God while also retaining an awareness of the limitations of embodied, contextual particularity. Trauma-sensitive theology seeks to honor the multiple commitments identified by Blumenthal and share in the honorable task of holding and exploring the boundary between the wisdom and potential for rejuvenation contained in our religious traditions and the real pain and suffering that results from traumatic wounding and response. The four primary commitments of trauma-sensitive theology and praxis, enumerated originally in the introduction, are worth repeating here: the priority of bodily experience, full acceptance of trauma narratives, natural given-ness of human psychological multiplicity, and faith in the robust resiliency of trauma survivors. These commitments directly intersect with the theological loci of theological anthropology, ecclesiology, theological ethics, hamartiology, imago Dei, trinity, ontology, pneumatology, creation, soteriology, and eschatology. Even through a cursory reflection and naming of connections between the primary commitments and theological categories, there are few theological loci exempt from direct engagement with the primary commitments of constructing a trauma-sensitive theology and pastoral care praxis. Because all areas of theological reflections are related and linked, we could proceed with the primary commitments as our framework; however, following the traditional journey of systematic theology also illustrates the path from original goodness through traumatic disruption into resiliency and attunement.

THE GROUND AND BE/ING:[3] AN ONTOLOGY

For the multitude of us who are not naturally inclined towards and excited by philosophical language and concepts, terms like "ontology" or "metaphysics" tend to make our eyes glaze over and feelings of overwhelm surface. We can even think that these areas of reflection and thoughtfulness don't really matter. While I empathize with the feeling, response, and thought, I also

2. Ibid., 3–4.

3. My use of "be/ing" is a link to Mary Daly's notion of be-ing as a verb rather than a noun. Her movement from the substance of nouns to the activity of verbs is an important and creative shift away from a purely substance orientation and towards a dynamic, process, active, fluid understanding of the divine. Mary Daly, *Beyond God the Father*.

believe that considering these questions is important because it establishes the bounds of possibility in our thinking and the overarching guidelines of what can be possible in our lives and world. In his highly influential *Systematic Theology*, Paul Tillich writes, "The ontological question is: What is being itself? What is that which is not a special being or a group of beings, not something concrete or something abstract, but rather something which is always thought implicitly, and sometimes explicitly, if something is said to *be*?"[4] In other words, what do we think and what can we confess when we think about what makes up our reality in its most foundational or elemental level? What, ultimately, does everything we can see, feel, and imagine come down to? Tillich "distinguishes four levels of ontological concepts: (1) the basic ontological structure which is the implicit condition of the ontological question; (2) the elements which constitute the ontological structure; (3) the characteristics of being which are the conditions of existence; and (4) the categories of being and knowing."[5] These four levels—structure, elements, characteristics, and categories—build on one another and help us explore the implicit notions that direct and order our experiences in the world. For the construction of trauma-sensitive theology and care, the ontological question shapes how we think about what is going on in traumatic response and what kinds of intervention are most helpful. For instance (and utilizing established ontologies), if we choose a substance ontology, then we are more inclined towards a final goal. If we choose a process ontology, we are more likely to focus on the dynamic process of wounding, response, and resiliency. Plainly stated, do we focus on what we see or the processes that formed what we see—or something else?

The question of "being," as Tillich notes, is not a specifically theological question but one of which theologians must be aware. It is not specifically theological in that it is typically not a central concern of theologians or those in congregational leadership. Nevertheless, how we consider these questions of being significantly impact our theological articulations. Is being a substance, a consciousness, an action? Shall we consider God the "ground of being" (Tillich), personal, or something more? Is all that is "One," monolithic, monovocal, monobiological? These questions came into focus for me in a conversation with a Bible scholar during my doctoral work. As she and I enjoyed our friendship, the conversation turned to how we personally conceptualized and related to God. As a New Testament

4. Tillich, *Systematic Theology*, vol. 1, 162.
5. Ibid., 164.

scholar, she was comforted by relating to God as a personal God who was imaged with qualities of intimacy, relationality, and care, like that of a parent. Given her context, her position made sense to me even though it differed from my own. As a religion and science and trauma scholar, the idea of a personal God seems far too limiting to my sensibilities. I needed a God that could transcend the limitations of personhood while still remaining intimately involved and engaged in all dimensions of life—human, animal, plant, the whole of the ecosystem. That conversation in conjunction with my understanding of process theology, chemistry, and ecology planted an ontological question: "What if the structure of being was energy itself?" What happens, theologically, relationally, psychologically, if we start to consider energy and the flow of energy through all life as the presence of the Divine in, with, for, and more than us?

If we explore the idea of energy as the foundational structure of all that is, then the second level, the elements of being, would include energy as bonded/ordered or as free/fluid. Bonded or ordered energy has the potential to manifest in matter. Energy can remain fluid serving as a conduit among clusters of bonded energy now in concrete forms. Bonded energy, like free energy, remains dynamic and engaging within its form as ordered matter. Ordered-ness does not mean static. All states of matter retain a dynamic quality. Bonded energy can organize into matter that forms my brain and body, my cat, the chair supporting my body as I write, the computer I am using, or the book you are reading. All that we see is, at its most basic, a complex, highly organized conglomeration of matter formed by bonded energy.

Once bonded or ordered energy transfers into matter, the question of relationality rises more acutely, though not anew. Relationality, a primary characteristic of being, is the quality of the dynamic conduit of fluid energy that connects all matter, living, organic, and non-organic. All that *is* is in relationship within itself and with all other forms of matter (to various degrees). The greater the connection between entities of bonded energy into matter, the greater potential exists to influence through those connections. It is the connection between and among, facilitated through the flow of free, non-bonded energy that links all be/ings of all complexities. This means that the distinction between me, my cat, and a rock is primarily a function of the complexity of the form of our bonded energy as matter, the degrees of relational connection, and capacity for influence available to each of us through free, non-bonded energy. The capacity to influence is especially important for constructing a trauma-sensitive theology and pastoral care praxis. As we will discuss more fully in the section on sin, the capacity to influence parts of self or others is our relational power and relational power is a function of the flow of free energy that links matter and organisms.

The characteristic of relationality can be considered via a great variety of categories of being. Categories of being can be considered as topics for reflection on the existence or essence of being or as spectrum that includes a variety of positions or points of reflection and experience. The categories of being specifically related to constructing a trauma-sensitive theology and care praxis include the spectrums of multiplicity/singularity, holism/atomism, constructive/destructive, and resonance/dissonance. Multiplicity/singularity point to the degree of recognized variety within an entity or organism. Do I view myself as a singular being or as composed of a variety of parts that each have their own function? Holism/atomism relates to how one views and attends to an entity or organism. Do I focus and curate my intention of care to the wellbeing of a system as a whole or do I focus on one component of the system? The spectrum category of constructive/destructive explores the addition or removal of relational connections or components of matter. The query is not correlative to value in that all construction is "good" and destruction is "bad"; rather, it is cultivating a curiosity of when addition facilitates healthy fulfillment and when removal facilitates health. The spectrum of resonance/dissonance honors degrees of attunement and harmony. To what extent am I in clear attunement or disconnected tension with the dimensions of self, other entities and organisms in the world, and the presence and flow of divine energy? Does the energy that is me vibrate with the same frequency, in harmony, or in dissonance with an other? The categories of being and spectrums of relationality are windows or lenses for reflection on the quality of the relational flow of energy within a person's be/ing, connections with others (human, non-human creatures, organic life, and inorganic entities), and the divine.

Considering an energy centered ontology, as distinct from a substance or process ontology or metaphysics, opens avenues for trauma-sensitive theology because it curates space for the wisdom of intuition and honors the felt sense of connection, disruption, and risk. If the base of what *is* is energy, how does that resonate with the understanding of the universe offered through the disciplines of the physical sciences? Does it make sense in terms of re-cycling of matter through life and death, consumption and defecation, or metabolism? What about the affective resonance that is felt via empathy and our mirror neurons? How about the spiritual experience of hearing the "still, small voice" or feeling the presence of God in our midst? Does conceptualizing our interactions as connections of free energy capable of influencing another entity or organism in ways that facilitate vitality and harmony or ways that contribute to harm and wounding assist us in cultivating wise compassion?

GOD, DIVINE PRESENCE: A THEOLOGY

When we engage in God talk, it is helpful to begin from a place of humility, reverence, and openness with an awareness that anything and everything we claim to know about God is limited and incomplete. Awareness of our limitations in imagination, conceptualization, articulation, and imagery does not mean that we cannot claim anything; it is simply an honest reckoning with the limitations and contextualization of human experience. "God is greater."[6] This simple proclamation points us to an awareness that the divine is more than our images, fears, shame, strengths, conceptualizations, or traditions. When faced with the clarity that anything we say about the divine is limited, some have opted to only claim what we cannot say. This approach, apophatic or negative theology, is an attempt to guard against the appearance of certainty about God that morphs the divine into a knowable or possess-able subjectivity. The tension of saying something without reducing the divine to the limits of human experience or imagination is an underlying challenge anytime we engage in corporate or individual theological formation. Nevertheless, there is value in exploring how we consider divine presence in our lives, communities, and the world.

The two areas of God talk most consequential to the development of a theological system and confession that cares for the wounds of trauma and facilitates resiliency are divine relationality, which centers on an exploration of the doctrine of the trinity within a Christian framework, and divine power. The doctrine of the Trinity has two main dimensions: the imminent trinity and the economic trinity. The imminent trinity focuses on the relationships among the persons of the Trinity while the economic trinity describes the relationship and function of each person in relation to the world. While the word "trinity" is nowhere in Bible (Christian Testament or Hebrew Bible), the theological concept of the trinity signifies the relational

6. The motto of Archbishop Antje Jackelén, Church of Sweden, excerpted from 1 John 3:18–20.

connections among God ("first person"),[7] Logos or Christ ("second person" who is incarnate in the person Jesus), and Spirit ("third person"). Within the Gospel narratives, the image of the baptism of Jesus with the dove of the Spirit descending and alighting upon him with the proclamation of parental-type pleasure and satisfaction by God illustrates the harmonious connection among the members of the Trinity. The picture is one of loving, attuned relationality in which each "person" is uniquely themselves with their own gifts and attributes and also deeply connected with each other. It is a vision of fully attuned community in a state of optimal relationality. The economic trinity connotes the function, role, or responsibility of each "person" in relationship with world, specifically humanity. This distinction is indicated in our language of God in terms of creator, redeemer, sustainer. These terms are centered on the relationship of each dimension of the divine to human life, faith, and history. They indicate God-with-us rather than God-in-Godself.

If we take the triune God as a model for optimal relationality that holds space for individual distinctions while also generating a nurturing and vivifying community, we glimpse a way of being in relation to self and others that reveals the best of healthy boundaries and altruism. It is a vision of cohesive multiplicity in which the difference is beloved, distinction is additive to the potential for connections of care and joy, and the sharing of vision does not mean an automatic reduction to sameness. In the framework and language of IFS, the imminent trinity is the paradigm and pinnacle of Self leadership and the economic trinity can be a model for unburdened "parts" when extrapolated for human being. For the construction of a trauma-sensitive theology, the doctrine of the trinity as a vision of cohesive multiplicity in optimal relationality is a powerful source of resiliency and resource for imaging right relationship.

The second element of the doctrine of God of particular significance for the construction and articulation of trauma-sensitive theology and praxis is the area of divine power. Divine power is a central proposition in the unfolding of systematic theology; the answer affirmed to the query of divine power establishes the main direction available for later journeying. The most common understanding of divine power is that "God is omnipotent, all-powerful, and mighty." The notion of the omnipotence of God

7. The word "person" is in quotation marks to both honor the theological language employed by the tradition while also noting that the notion of personhood when applied to the members of the Trinity can lead to a reductionist impression that the "persons" of the Trinity are akin to human persons.

establishes both the quality and intensity of God's influence in the world. Quality refers to the felt sense of the influence (care, mutuality, dominion, etc.) and intensity refers to power of the influence (power over, power with, power on behalf of, etc.). Omnipotence generally connotes a dominating power in which the will of the one exerting power is unmatched and effective. Colloquially, this theological position related to the power of God shows up in phrases like "Everything that happens is God's will." Providing comfort to some and torment to others, the omnipotence of God clearly and unambiguously places responsibility for all that happens in the world at the foot of the omnipotent God. This understanding of divine power is most prevalent and most dangerous in its role of contributing to subsequent non-consensual uses of dominating power in which the agency of the one is the solely considered. Additionally, it is frequently critiqued as an erasure of the notion of humanity's free will and agency to make choices for and in our lives and relationships.

If omnipotence is problematic, what is an alternative? The most compelling alternative for me comes from process philosophy and theology.[8] Process theology, which emerges from a metaphysics that differs significantly from the substance metaphysic that fuels the doctrine of omnipotence, offers a vision of divine power and agency that honors mutuality and choice over domination. God's power, in process theology, is in crafting creative, life affirming options for each organism and then "luring" each of us towards the most healthy and fulfilling choice available within the constraints of our existence. God does not force the choice but rather self-limits God's power and influence to engage each of us in co-generation of our life and world. For process, God offers a number of choices to us in each moment with a great variety. Some of the choices are better than others and God does have a preference; however, God does not force the preference but waits with expectation for our choice. Once we make our choice, God takes it into God's self, is impacted by it, and offers the next path.

The process offering of divine power and agency does not render God impotent; rather, it creates space for a degree of mutuality, consent, and human agency in the unfolding of life in the world. The shift toward a process understanding of divine power, and away from the doctrine of omnipotence, is important in relation to trauma in (at least) two respects. First, it lets God off the hook as the sole agent responsible for traumatizing violations and woundings. If God is omnipotent, then God bears all the weight

8. See Alfred North Whitehead, *Process and Reality* (Toronto: Macmillan, 1929).

of the most horrendous acts in our world. Given the prevalence of the omnipotence model, it is no wonder that experiences of traumatic wounding
and loss are among the most significant reasons why people abandon their
religious traditions and communities. The theo-logic[9] is that if God has all
the power and exerts God's own will then everything that happens is the
choice of God. If God chooses, for God's own pleasure or agenda, massive
suffering, as evidenced in grand scale in the Holocaust and in small scale
in the sudden or violent deaths of loved ones, then God is unloving and
unworthy of worship. Additionally, this articulation of divine power risks
positing God as the supreme perpetrator of trauma and violence. However,
if God self-limits divine power and agency, then traumatizing experiences
in life are not necessarily the will and pleasure of God. If fact, these events
could be antithetical to the desires of God but occur because human agents
fail to follow the "lure" of God and cause God grief and sadness in empathetic attunement with us. God, in this vision, is actively and compassionately involved with all of life in the world. God grieves and rejoices
alongside us as we journey through our life in a multitude of relationships.
God persistently hopes for the fulfilling health of all of creation while also
knowing that it must be chosen, not forced.

The second important shift is key in cultivating a theology that can
facilitate recovery and resiliency rather than retraumatize survivors. It is
the move from "power over" as a unilateral expression of domination to
a model of "power with" as an expression of consent and shared desire for
fulfillment. For individuals and communities who have viscerally experienced the harmful consequences of unilateral power that erases consent,
the doctrine of divine omnipotence is not good news; rather, it is the source
of traumatic injury. As Mary Daly helped us realized, the way we image
and talk about God and God's power in the world matters. As she famously
noted, "if God is male, then the male is God."[10] Her point is that when we
image God as male, with varying degrees of awareness, we begin to grant
males the power associated with God. By extension, if God's power is *all*
powerful, unilateral, dominating, and definitive, then it further justifies human use of power that is unilateral, dominating, and non-consensual. This
image of power can then be coupled with theologies of submission of those
with less social power with dangerous consequences and traumatic injury.

9. A wonderful term I first encountered in Catherine Keller's work. Keller, *On the
Mystery.*

10. Daly, *Beyond God the Father,* 19.

The image of divine power offered by process theology is an antidote to the harmful consequences of omnipotence. Relational, luring/inviting, consensual power enables the agency of all parties and generates healthy attachments and connections that attend to mutuality and care. If human power as an extension of divine power is wielded with self-restraint, wisdom, and compassion, then power can contribute to resiliency and survivors of traumatic wounding have a theologically grounded resource for reclaiming agency and courage in the task of processing trauma. God is no longer the ultimate source of wounding but is now the source of care and agency. God desires recovery and resiliency, grieves with the experience of wounding, and offers options towards fullness of life. God's relational power is one of gentle molding and guiding.

CRAFTING A GARDEN: A THEOLOGY OF CREATION

"In the beginning . . ." These words open both the book of Genesis and the gospel according John. "In the beginning God created the heavens and earth."[11] "In the beginning was the Word."[12] The parallel structure is intentional as the writer of John sought to call forth one of the ancient narratives of creation and link the creative power of God to the power of Jesus. Stories of beginnings have a special kind power in and of themselves. They set the stage for all that is to come, establish a range of possibilities, and orient us in time and space. They also determine whose vision of the beginnings will take a formative position within the community. Narratives of beginnings can either mirror each other in an effort to draw the authority given to one into the other or they can offer competing world views and priorities. For instance, in my current context, the narratives of "beginnings" that continue to be the object of cultural battle are the scientific narrative of the Big Bang and the religious narratives of creation. While there are many interesting avenues for this particular fight for cultural power including attention to the intention and area of inquiry reflected by each narrative, that specific narrative power struggle is not the focus of this conversation. I name it simply to acknowledge what is at stake in beginnings and the positions more recent narratives take in reference to more established ones. Whether in resonance or dissonance, all narratives require interpretation. The lenses we use for interpretation have a profound impact on our conclusions we

11. Genesis 1:1.
12. John 1:1.

come to and how we communicate. Recall that the hermeneutical lenses for trauma-sensitive theology are the hermeneutics of alterity, multiplicity, empathy, and accountability which received direct attention in chapter 4. The Christian doctrine of creation is most commonly articulated as *creatio ex nihilo*, creation out of nothing, is an outflow of a system based on a substance metaphysic, reinforces an omnipotent understanding of divine power and reflects a conflation of the distinct traditions found within the Pentateuch (Torah or the first five books of the Bible) and Wisdom literature within the Hebrew Bible.

I will confess that during my high school and college years I was a very devout and conservative Christian. I name this time as a confession because looking back at that period of my faith development I can recognize some of the ways in which my young understanding of faith and devotion led to a strict adherence that was, at times, unkind and ignorant of larger social dynamics. The combination of my spiritual fidelity, analytical mind, draw towards theology, and need to fit all the pieces together in a nice and neat way paved the way for a shocking revelation, at the time, that the biblical text was not univocal. I recall quite clearly my undergraduate class in theology in which the professor made the bold (or so I thought at the time) statement that the creation narratives of Genesis 1 and 2–3 emerged from two different oral traditions and could not be merged together into a seamless whole. I remember sitting at my desk long after class ended going through those three chapters clause by clause in the effort to merge them. I did not succeed in my task that day but I did learn the valuable lesson that the sacred texts that had been supporting my life in the world for years were in fact far more complicated and intriguing than I had previously realized. That day in class I began to have an appreciation, which grew into loving fascination, with the alterity and multiplicity of voices, needs, and intentions within the Christian scriptures. Scripture was no longer a static document that functioned as a catalyst for my personal spirituality, regardless of how literally life sustaining that approach was at the time. This awareness, coupled with a remarkable Ash Wednesday ritual in which I began to come into awareness of feminism, was the start of an expansive shift towards the rich variety and meaning available within sacred texts and practices.

The stories of the beginning in Genesis 1 and in Genesis 2–3 are not scientific accounts of astrophysics or cosmology. To reduce them to a scientific claim would be to miss their great significance entirely. Rather, they represent the presence of alterity, the beauty of multiplicity, the comfort of empathy, and the hope for accountability in the midst of living in a foreign and dangerous land. It is well established by biblical scholars who have devoted their professional lives to the study of these ancient sacred texts in their English translations and original languages that there are four distinct oral traditions reflected in the Pentateuch: the Yahwist, the Elohist, the Deuteronomist, and the Priestly.[13] The creation narrative in Genesis 1 reflects the Priestly voice and the one in Genesis 2–3 emerges from the Yahwist tradition. With different communities and intentions, the Priestly account emphasizes the generation of order from chaos with a clear almost rhythmic cadence of creature generation while the Yahwist tradition embraces our relationship to earth and intimate connections with divine presence.

Two important moments from the Priestly account resonate with me for the formation of trauma-sensitive work. The first is in the opening verses:

> When Elohim *began to create the heaven and the earth—(2) the earth was* tohu va bohu ("waste and wild") *and darkness was upon the face of* tehom ("oceanic deep") *and* ruach ("Spirit") *was pulsing over the face of the waters—(3) then* Elohim *said let there be light. . .*[14]

Catherine Keller's translation and beautifully evocative meaning making highlights several key terms in the Hebrew as a means of opening up our imaginative engagement with a well known passage. As she illuminates in the text, the Earth was a watery, deep, wild, dark, and untamed space with the Spirit pulsating and vibrating over the surface when Elohim began the work of crafting the boundless energy into the focusing of light. The watery chaos of the abyss was not something to be feared or exiled by Elohim; rather, it was the matter available to form something beautiful. This viewing of the opening of Genesis 1 has the capacity to radically shift our imaginations and faith. Rather than fearing the chaos deep within each of our beings, what if we welcomed the chaos as the energy and matter for creation? In resonance I recall a quote from Nietzsche gifted to me by a mentor when I was writing my dissertation, "I say unto you: One must still have chaos in oneself to be able to give birth to a dancing star."[15] Creation of worlds, a life,

---

13. Brueggemann, *An Introduction to the Old Testament*, 9.

14. Translation from Keller, *On the Mystery*, 48. See also Keller, *Face of the Deep*.

15. Fredrich Nietzsche, *Thus Spoke Zarathustra*.

or oneself does not occur out of nothing; it happens when we embrace the messy chaos, engage our creativity, and draw on the energy of the chaos to create from what is present. Static, clean, perfection is not the aim . . . nor is it possible in this wild, deeply fluid world.

The second moment is the self-designated multiplicity of Elohim in the creation of human beings. "Then Elohim said, 'Let *us* make human beings in *our* image, in *our* likeness'" (Gen 1:26, emphasis added). While it is an inauthentic reach to ascribe the plurality of first person pronouns in God's proclamation to make humanity in God's own image as an indicator of the doctrine of the Trinity,[16] it is interesting and helpful to pay attention to the spaces that open up through the multiplicity indicated in the "us" and "our" of Elohim. What shifts in our theological rendering of "normal" when multiplicity is affirmed by God in Elohim's self identification? One of the first areas of movement that comes to mind is the theological construct of the "oneness" of God. When "One" is the paradigm, it necessarily moves communities towards thought patterns and social constructions that reflect the "One." Theologian Laurel Schneider traces the history and function of "the One"[17] to establish and reinforce systems of unilateral power and agency while highlighting what is at stake when oneness is the sole option for authentic faith and community identity. She writes,

> Oneness and unity, like all abstractions (including the abstraction of divine multiplicity) are vulnerable to the fallacy of misplaced concreteness. Their usefulness makes it easy to forget that they are concepts placed upon reality to sort its ontological multiplicity. No matter how many times we may wish to lift our gaze from the cacophony of embodied existence toward the serenity of unifying concepts in the hope of bringing closure to the world's actual unruly shiftiness, the attempt to construct a summary "after all" fails . . . Without the multiplicity of matter, unity slips into ideology and begins to dream—noisily—of reductions, closures, and totality . . . Although unity (even more than oneness) is an ingredient of sanity for human beings, neither idea is adequate to conceptualize divinity, or world. It is out of the logic of the One that Hell's eternity was made, to squash the real multiplicity of divinity and world into a basement closet of ice, and so to pretend that it is

16. Gunkel, *Genesis*, 112.

17. "[T]he One" is Schneider's designation for the power granted to and through theological traditions of monotheism.

"in charge of the world" . . . This dream of the One is a denial of incarnation and a serious error in theological thinking.[18]

As a conversation partner to the moment in the Priestly creation narrative in which Elohim honors the more-than-oneness within the Divine Creator, Schneider helps us clarify what is to gain and what is at stake in whether or not we take into our creativity and faith the "us" and "our" of God. When we fail to honor multiplicity in the divine or in creation and lead with a conception of normative singularity of identity, persons, communities, animals, or apples misses out on the vast array of what is present in existing matter. Moreover, it threatens removes us from "the cacophony of embodied existence" in which resides the messiness of the actual world—the world that is beautifully crafted from the wild and watery deep . . . and is good!

The Yahwist account provides a different ordering of creation and is more intimate and connected to the Earth than the Priestly. For the Yahwist, which is the oldest of the four traditions dating to tenth century BCE[19], the connection of humanity to the Earth is a central emphasis. In this creation narrative, YHWH finds the earth present with springs of water that emerge from the ground but lacking plant life, animal life, or anyone to care and tend the earth. So, God tenderly and with care forms "adam" from the "adamah" or the human from the humus. The word play of the Yahwist connects human beings to the ground of the earth. The intimacy of YHWH's care/full molding of the human, filling the human with life giving breath, planting of the garden to provide shelter and nutrition, and then offering the human animal companions indicates an intention towards deep care, connection, and relationality among God, human beings, the environment, and animals. This component of the Yahwist narrative draws focus to the importance of bodily integrity and relationships of compassionate care. God, in this rendering, is not a dispassionate or distant presence, rather God walks among the creatures and life in the garden with the joy and expectation of relationship.

The creation narratives offered by the Priestly and Yahwist traditions are only two of four depictions of creation found within the Hebrew Bible (the other two are in Psalm 104 and Job 38–42). They each offer a vision that comports with the awareness, needs, and oral traditions of the communities from which they emerge. The differences do not necessitate a crisis of faith

18. Schneider, *Beyond Monotheism*, 200.

19. Brueggemann, *Introduction to the Old Testament*, 8–9.

nor a reflexive protection of the "unity" of Scripture; rather, they offer us a fuller appreciation of how early communities of faith interacted with divine presence as they experienced faith in the world. Additionally, the variations point to the presence of options in how people of faith reflect on divine power and degree of relationality between God and creation. There is not just *one* path of faithful engagement with God in the text. There are many avenues for engaging with divine power and relational presence that honor the traditions of our sacred texts and point to the presence of diversity, alterity, and multiplicity within the very narrative fabric of our scriptures, faith, and understanding of existence and being.

6

Traumatic Disruption

The vision of utopias, whether in our historical or theological past or in our imagined and hoped for futures, are seductive. The narratives and hopes of existence in a peaceful, tranquil environment in which everyone has "enough" and all living things are free from pain, discord, violence, and death are a recurring theme in human imaginative and social life. From the Garden of Eden to the paradise of Heaven, utopias stand as both lost inheritance and promised future. It is as if there is some deep recognition that life is not as it can be, should be, or was. Real life is more tenuous, vulnerable, and ephemeral than our imagined utopias. The stark contrast between our best possible selves in the best possible world and the reality of our lives points to our deep intuitive wisdom that human beings have an innate capacity for good and also fail to live up to fullest capacity resulting in injury and wounding to ourselves and others. The "goodness" proclaimed by the Priestly Elohim at the conclusion of each day, including the day in which human beings are made in the image of the divine "us," in combination with the deep and loving relationality of the Yahwist's garden provides a vision of creation as fundamentally good when unburdened.

IN THE IMAGE: A THEOLOGICAL ANTHROPOLOGY

Questions centering on the fundamental identity of human beings, individually or as a species, are perennial and often reflect the knowledge and perspective of the times, specifically the vantage point of the person/s asking the questions. Who are we? What makes us different than other mammals and why? How should we make sense of humanity's treatment of each other and the world? These are the questions of theological anthropology. When we focus our reflection of theological anthropology in light of traumatic wounding, response, and resiliency, several themes emerge: the reflection of divine multiplicity in human beings, the capacity for resiliency and connected attunement, and the vital importance of holding the balance between similarity and distinction without reduction to universality on one end and dissolution of shared humanity on the other. Rather than turning to religious creation narratives to reveal the "how" of humanity's existence, theological anthropology focuses attention to creation narratives and other significant texts and passages to get a glimpse into "who" we can be as individuals and as a species. What is the capacity of our underlying nature before we experienced wounding and harm? Are we merely "rotgut sinners" or "totally depraved" doomed to live out of our most wounded parts? Or are we creatures of wondrously beautiful, complex multiplicity carrying both the weight of the burdens of past wounding and the resources for compassionate attunement and care for the needs of our own wounded parts and the injuries of others?

Previous chapters have included descriptions of the Internal Family Systems model of psychotherapy. While the IFS framework gives us a template for therapeutic work, it also, perhaps more engagingly, provides a psychological anthropology that is significantly useful for exploring theological anthropology.[1] The key components of IFS that have the potential to connect to theological anthropology are internal multiplicity as normative and adaptive, the presence of Self in every person (or organism), and the importance of cultivating and nourishing healthy internal attachments and relationships among parts and between Self and all parts. When we venture into the space of theological anthropology, it is not enough for psychological models to "work," they also must resonate and have confluence with our theological wisdoms.

Let us return to the Priestly account of the formation of human beings in Genesis 1: 26–28a. "Then God said, 'Let us make humankind in our image, in our likeness, so that they may rule over the fish in the sea and the birds in the sky, over the livestock and all the wild animals, and over all the

---

1. While I utilize IFS as a lens for developing a theological anthropology in this work, the use of models of human multiplicity have enjoyed a recent surge in the creative thinking of theologians. Most notably, Pamela Cooper-White has several texts available that explore the frameworks offered by relational psychoanalysis to discuss human multiplicity and form a model for the practice of pastoral care and counseling. Cooper-White, *Many Voices;* Cooper-White, *Braided Selves.*

creatures that move along the ground. So God created humankind in God's own image, in the image of God they were created, male and female. God blessed them." Our conversation about the doctrine of God and the Trinity focused on the multiplicity of persons within the imminent Trinity as an example of optimal relationality unfettered by relational wounding. The divine plurality of Elohim's "our" is significant for theological anthropology when noted that the writer highlights that human beings are made in "image" and "likeness." The question of the exact character of the "image" and "likeness" has vacillated and enjoyed a variety of answers over time. The human characteristics identified as "image" and "likeness" have included, among other options, consciousness, rationality, dominion/domination, and bipedal locomotion. In each of these responses, the leading question is "what makes human beings distinct from all other species?" Rather than taking our lead from our awareness of human attributes, what if we explore the optimal relationality present in the imminent Trinity as the source of our embodied reflection of divine multiplicity?

The divine multiplicity of the Trinity exemplifies attuned, compassionate, clear, curious, courageous, grounded, calm, confident, creative, connected relationality. These qualities are reflected in the characteristics of the human Self, from the IFS model, and the religious aspirations for people (i.e., fruits of the Spirit, etc.) across traditions. Could the model of divine multiplicity in optimal (Self-led) relationality provide an adaptive lens for theological reflection on the human being? Additionally, how would this shift facilitate the growth of healthy communities and support recovery from traumatic wounding? When we take the combination of the natural presence of human psychological multiplicity and the optimal relationality offered through Self-leadership as the inheritance offered to human beings via our creation in the image of Elohim, we begin to shift our awareness of human possibility. It is a shift away from viewing human beings as organisms of static, one-ness who repeatedly fail to meet the ideals and expectations of perfection and towards a complex, dynamic community of parts that hold burdens but also the potential for healing attunement and attachment to the wounding parts within and among us.

Another way to imagine the inheritance of attuned, trusting, and loving relationality within each person through Imago dei/Self leadership is Rita Nakashima Brock's offering of "original grace."[2] Original grace is a foil to traditional notions original sin as a foundational description of human

2. Brock, *Journeys By Heart.*

beings. For Brock, original grace is our "ontological relational existence" and the means through which a heart and life may be restored and nourished. As a counter image of humanity's fundamental disposition, original grace is not blind to the reality of sin in human individuals and communities but offers the active hope of recovery, resiliency, and reconciliation that allows us to take an active role in our relationships and communities. Additionally, the concept of original grace permits a full range of emotional responses to life in the world without designating some as sinful or evil and allows people to acknowledge injustice and violation with legitimate anger that can lead to self-acceptance and compassion. In other words, Brock's concept of original grace mirrors the concept of Self as the fundamental capacity of human beings to accept and honor all dimensions of who we are and move towards acceptance and care of all parts of our multiple self. "Such openness means that the terrifying and destructive factors of life are also taken into the self, a self that then requires loving presence to be restored to grace. Finding our heart requires a loving presence who helps the search, who is not afraid of the painfulness of the search, and who can mirror back our buried and broken heart, returning us to a healing memory of our earliest pain and need for love. This loving presence and healing memory carry the profoundest meanings of forgiveness and remembrance."[3] The original grace present in Self reassures us and roots us in the hope of resiliency and faith that we are, in fact, fundamentally "enough." The deep assurance that our internal wellspring fosters attuned attachment via a deep connection to the optimal relationality of God gifts us with the courage, creativity, curiosity, and compassion to connect with all parts of who we are and with others in our midst.

Honoring the divine presence of original grace and Self in each person (and organism) does not negate the importance of care/fully attending to the distinctions of our lived experience. While Self and Self energy may draw from the eternal well of divine energy, all of our parts are specific to the individual and their life circumstances. Many of our parts exist in our psychological world with wounds or burdens from specific life experiences, some traumatic and many non-traumatic. Parts that may have emerged within our lives in cared-for environments and once-held feelings and beliefs of sufficient care and worth can become wounded and shift their operating sense of the world to one of fear and fierce protection. While there are no "bad" parts, sometimes the heavy burdens, no-longer-useful

3. Ibid., 17.

beliefs, or dysfunctional strategies employed by parts can lead to discord or additional wounding of self or others. The specific life experiences that result in wounds and burdens have profound influence on how we care for self and relate with others in the world. These distinctions, experiences, and particularities cannot be overlooked or minimized without peril. When we try to ignore parts of us or specific parts in others, we only succeed in further injuring and exiling those very parts. On the other hand, if we can feel into the resources available in Self, we can protect, soothe, and comfort the hurting, controlling, or fleeing parts in us. Offering attuned, caring, loving attachment and relationship from Self to our parts does not make them "go away" rather it eases the wound, deescalates the need for protection, and allows parts to reclaim their original, vital, and creative role in our life. Like the "persons" of the Trinity, our parts each have a relational role to play within our own "imminent" psychological and embodied being and have an "economic" function in relating to other beings in the world. When we are better able to facilitate harmony, love, and grace within, we are more equipped to offer harmony, love, and grace in the world. Recognition of our internal distinctions, when unburdened and recovered from wounding, expand our capacity for recognizing and cultivating empathy for the distinctions within others and in our society. Alterity and difference are no longer perceived as threat or belittled but can be honored as additional gifts for crafting our society. The ways in which we respond to alterity within and outside of set the bounds of what is possible in restoring health and crafting communities of equality and vitality.

HUMAN POWER AND AGENCY

At its most basic, power is the capacity to exert influence. While the definition of power may be short and sweet, how people choose to utilize their power is anything but. All organisms and entities have some measure of power. Power exists in a range of forms and with a great variety of intensity. Power, whether divine power, human agency, or ecological, is not a have/don't have binary. The question regarding power is not "Do you have power or do you not have power?" Rather, it is "What forms of power do you have access to and in what intensity?" The claim that all entities in existence have some measure of power is a reflection of the ontology offered in the previous chapter. Power is an existential reflection of the ontological free/unbounded energy that connects us to ourselves, one another, the world, and, the source of all energy, the divine or God. Power, in and of itself, is neither good nor bad; it is relatively value neutral. The valuation of power is derived from its usage.

All forms of power are ultimately relational. The connections used to exert influence are connections between or among. Socially, they are the connections we have to others within our social group, the connections between and among various social groups, and the systems that groups establish in order to influence the rules and norms that govern large collectives of society. Interpersonally, the connections are closer or more intimate. We each have some measure of power to influence those with whom we are in personal or professional relationships. The power each of us wields in relationships varies according to the form of relationship or the momentary dynamics of the relationship. Parents and employers generally exert more influence over children and employees, respectively, than the other way around. However, the momentary dynamics of the relationship may shift the power structure within a particular dyad resulting in moments where children or employees wield significant influence. Internally and intrarelationally, Self or various parts can hold significant power in the overall system. Managers can run a person's internal system for decades. Firefighters or escape artists can over take a system in distress. The power of exiles can organize a person's entire life in avoidance of feelings of shame or powerlessness. Self can also establish trusting and caring leadership and obtain the power to lead and protect a person's internal system.

Agency, human and other, reflects our capacity to choose how we use the power we have. Whether we cultivate awareness of the forms and intensities of our social, interpersonal, and intrapersonal connections of influence and power or choose to live unaware of these connections, we all exert our personal power and influence every day that we live and some of us continue to have the power to influence after we die. How we choose to use our relational power is significant. In each moment of relational connection, even if it is truly only a moment, do we choose to use our power in a way that honors the alterity and life of the other with empathy and care or do we choose to assert our power in a way that dishonors or harms? These choices hold additional weight when made by the person in the relational dyad with more social power. When the person with more social or relational power, whether interpersonal or systemic, uses their power to harm, injure, wound, or dishonor, they have abused their relational power.[4] When

---

4. I am grateful to Dr. Jim Poling for introducing me to the conceptual phrase "abuses

the person with more relational power uses their power to encourage towards health, and honors, cares for, or empathetically attunes to the person with less power, they have contributed to the vital health of relationality and honored the power of divine free energy in the world.

The choices human beings make in how we choose to use our relational power are often influenced by our personal theology of divine power and agency. If the character of divine power is unidirectional (God has power over the world but the world does not have the capacity to influence God), absolute, directive in that entities and organisms in the world have no choice, then human beings will reflect that understanding of power itself in their use of it. Human imitations of unidirectional, non-relational power necessarily lead to the atrophy of empathy, abandonment of compassion, and wounding of our persons, society, and the world. On the other hand, if the character of divine power is relational, open, secure enough to invite rather than command, and aimed toward empathetic attunement that honors the dignity of the other, then human agency will reflect this form and tone of relational power. Because relational power is fueled by the connections generated by the free energy of God, the character of the God we preach, teach, and place faith in will influence the ways in which each of us embodies power in our relational dyads and connections.

SIN, WOUNDING, AND THE ORIGINAL OFFENSE: A HAMARTIOLOGY

The theological category of sin has tremendous variation in the history of the church. For much of the history of Christian theology from the disciples of Jesus until recent decades, the majority of theologians were men with significant social relational power. As such, their understanding of how men sinned was defined as falling short of perfection or the glory of God and centered on the patterns of behaviors of individual men. These moral failings were indicative of the inheritance of sin, original sin. The robust longevity and ubiquity of the doctrine of original sin is largely reflective of the dominance of the systematic theological system of which it is but one piece. When God is distant and all powerful, divine agency is definitive and unilateral, creation automatically bends towards God's will, then

---

of power" in class and in his wonderful text. My use and expansion of his concept and phrase have been a cornerstone in my own reflection of abuse and trauma. Poling, *Abuse of Power*.

anything that displeases or fails to exhibit deference and claim any power is marked by pride and sin. Consequently, since the world is no longer the garden of perfection due to the disobedience of the first humans, with the first woman taking the bulk of the blame, then sin must be a characteristic of us all. The pieces all fit within a system of theological domination and unilateral power; however, this doesn't have to be the only or even best theological option.

The definition of sin that resonates most clearly for me in constructing a trauma-sensitive theology is: sin is the abuse of relational power. In relation to this definition of sin, "abuse" is used to designate an ab/use, or misuse, of relational power. Ab/use of relational power does not need to meet the criteria or severity of psychological or legal definitions of the word, though it may. I intentionally use this word to highlight the potential consequences of the misuse of our relational power in service to desires that ultimately cause harm or restrict well-being. This definition includes the the use of systemic, social, interpersonal, or intrapersonal power in a manner that reduces or leads to the "absence of well-being"[5] in self, others, society, or the ecological world. Sin as an/the abuses of relational power differs from other concepts in its ability to encompass the full range of the ways in which human beings injure and wound other persons, creatures, or the world. As such, it is a helpful frame for considering the established categories of interpersonal sin, systemic sin, moral sin, and ecological sin. Sin as the abuse of relational power is a lens for acknowledging the variety of ways in which human beings use our relational power to undermine well-being through mistreatment of each other, lack of caring attention towards all parts of ourselves, establishment and perpetuation of social structures that actively and passively harm communities, and the abandonment of our responsibility to care for "the fish in the sea and the birds in the sky and over every living creature that moves on the ground" (Gen 1:28b).

The vast web of each of our individual relational connections means that we all have some measure of response-ability to use our relational power in a way that facilitates well-being rather than ab/usive mistreatment. Those of us who were granted more access to social power by virtue of our place of birth and the resources available to us have a responsibility to become aware of our connections of power and utilize that power to do the smallest amount of harm possible while promoting the well-being of

---

5. The "absence of well being" is the criteria that" markes sin as sin" according to Marjorie Hewitt Suchocki. For more information see Suchocki, *The Fall to Violence*, 13.

as many as possible. Those of us who experience life on the underside of relational and social power structures are not exempt from the invitation to use relational power to promote well-being, even if the only connection available is between Self and a wounded exile, anxious manager, or impulsive escape artist within. All of us, from the leaders of nations to the smallest traumatized child, have some relational connection through which we can offer empathy, curiosity, and compassion. Our innate capacity, gifted to us through the free energy of the divine, for relational attuned connection can be used for fulfillment and harmonious well-being or to harm or disregard others for our own selfish gains or needs. Both choices are available to us in each moment of relationality with parts of self, others, the world, or God. Unfortunately, too often we choose harm over health out of our own burdens, misunderstandings, or wounds and we sin. We are all culpable at some point in our lives of misusing our relational power. We all "have sinned and fallen short" and the price owed by our abuses of relational power are too often death of relationship, injury to parts, or wounding of our collective relational webs of life.

Wounding and sin emerge from our own experiences of being on the receiving end of harm. When we experience harm from the presence of hurt or absence of care, a part of us is wounded, holds onto the experience on behalf of the system, and constructs a set of beliefs about life in the world that take the harm into account. We then begin living through parts enlisted in protecting us from experiencing that form of harm again. For example, if we are made fun of by peers, a part may take on the burden and belief that friends and community are risky. As a result, we may misuse our relational power to push people away in an attempt to secure our own sense of safety. If we are told that we will never amount to anything, a part may either believe the message and retreat from life or a part may overfunction to prove to everyone that we are successful in every area of life. The consequence of attempting to prove that you do, in fact, matter and can be successful may become an overarching strategy in life in which promoting oneself and acquiring resources by any means necessary becomes a dominant characteristic of life.

As a contrast to the theological doctrine of original sin, Sheila Kelley, founder of S Factor, convincingly argues for the importance of recognizing "original offenses."[6] Focusing on the category for the cultivation of feminine power, she proposes that feminine power is wounded initially through

6. Kelley, "Let's Get Naked."

an original offense in which girls first learn that there are different rules for girls than boys and that living in a girl's body is not as safe or acceptable as living in a boy's body. The learning that results from the original offense is replicated multiple times through life either through implicit socialization or sexualization, explicit "rules" for being a girl/woman, and/or traumatic violence. While many original offenses occur under the guise of protecting or educating girls on "proper" social behavior, this pedagogical shaming occurs in a social context that overly sexualizes women. While Kelley's focus is on the relationship between original offenses and the formative instructions guiding girls and women through social development, it is also illuminative of the dynamics present in a variety of lessons taken in by our early experiences and mirrors the developmental learnings through other original offenses we received in relation to race, class, ability, sexual orientation, etc. When we shift away from original sin towards original offenses as the source of our beliefs that result in later abuses of relational power, we generate distance from a model of sin that is highly problematic and often assigns culpability to those who are vulnerable while continuing to neglect the burdens that undergird harmful strategies for living. By refocusing on the concept of original offense, we gain space for compassion and empathy while also retaining connection to the original grace that is present in all living organisms and entities.

Sin as abuses of relational power rather than a given inheritance of humanity is important for survivors of traumatic wounding and those who offer care. First, when sin is named as a violation against the rules established by God or society, survivors of traumatic wounding too often internalize the violation as their fault as a means to maintain some measure of agency. Second, promoting the inherited sinfulness of all humanity risks minimizing the violation and impact of the abuse of power in which all "sin" is equally harmful. Third, if sin is an offense against God in which human beings "fall short of God's glory," then it shifts the party who experienced harm from the victim/survivor to God. It is then relationship with God that must be restored rather than the victim/survivor who is subsequently theologically erased and further wounded by the erasure. Shifting to a theology of sin as abuse of relational power re-centers attention and care to the one wounded and opens space for the need, opportunity, and capacity for restoration. Restoration is cultivating resiliency and repairing the wounds of the relational injury with or without restoring the relational connection between perpetrators and victim/survivors. Often recovery and resiliency means setting boundaries to protect from the parts of the perpetrator. Other times, it means facilitating honest acknowledgement and awareness of the burdened parts of the offender, reminding the person that they have resources of divine connection and original grace to repair the relationship between the perpetrating part of the person and their Self. This reconceptualization of sin coupled with the primary commitment to honor the natural multiplicity of human beings opens up significantly more options to facilitate health than available through other doctrines of sin.

JESUS, THE CHRIST: A CHRISTOLOGY

Perhaps the single most distinct theological question and response of Christian theology is the question of Jesus. Who is Jesus? What makes Jesus different than all other human beings and religious leaders or teachers? What is the relationship between Jesus and the persons of the Trinity? The question of Jesus the Christ is the central indicator of Christian theology and faith. So, who is Jesus or Christ for a trauma-sensitive theology? There are two primary trajectories for considering the theological importance of Christology: high Christologies and low Christologies. High Christologies emphasize the divinity of Christ and low Christologies focus on the incarnated Jesus. Like other theological choice points, Christology is largely influenced by other the character of other loci. Emphasis on the divinity of Christ follows the trajectory set by theologies of God's transcendence, omnipotence, and sin as separation. Christ's divinity, rather than humanity, is emphasized as a means of both connecting Christ to humanity so as to provide a path to remedy the chasm between who God created humanity to be and who we existentially are and as a strategy for keeping the divinity of Jesus the Christ untainted by the original sin that dooms human beings. Emphasis on the humanity of Jesus also functions as a component in the larger theological system that centers on divine imminence, relational power, and sin as moral failing. The humanity of Jesus, rather than divinity of the "second person," establishes Jesus as a human being who can fully understand the challenges of human life and community. Jesus "gets" us because Jesus is truly one of us . . . plus.

The theological question of how to make sense of the confession that Jesus the Christ is "fully God and fully human" has been perennial since the early Church counsels. The question of "how can Jesus be two in one?" mirrors the question of "how can God be three in one?" These concerns are amplified when we neglect the multiplicity of the divine, Jesus the Christ, and humanity. Through the lens of multiplicity, the two natures of Jesus the Christ become an opportunity for connection and model of internal harmony. Through the incarnation of Christ, the second person, as the embodied Jesus, we obtain a glimpse of the optimal relationality of true Self negotiating the challenges of embodied life in the world. Jesus, an embodied human being, takes on the full experience of humanity—including having parts that reflect the norms of his cultural experience and have the potential to be wounded and carry burdens associated with wounding. Jesus, as the incarnate Christ, also is fully led by Self and reflects a deep, unobstructed connection to the source of all Self energy, God.

For trauma-sensitive theology, Jesus is the fully Self-led human in which all parts of Jesus exist in right relationship with one another and Self, and relate to others in the world from a place of compassionate, courageous, clear, curiosity and attuned empathy. Jesus reveals the grace-filled potential of a life lived unconstrained by the beliefs generated though life's wounds and fears and the increasingly extreme strategies parts employ in attempts to keep us safe enough. The life of Jesus as recounted in the Gospels shows a Self-led life free from burdened and wounded parts. Jesus demonstrates how to live a Self-led life even in the midst of life's challenges, restrictions, and cultural biases. With caveats for the dimensions of Jesus that reflect the cultural norms of his era regarding gender and ethnicity rather than full attunement to and recognition of Self energy in all persons (e.g., Jesus' treatment of the Syrophoenician woman in Matthew 15:21–28) or the typical pressing of boundaries that mark human adolescence (e.g., Jesus' temple visit at age twelve in Luke 2:41–52), the Gospel accounts of the life and ministry of Jesus reflect a compassionate commitment to promoting multidimensional well-being and justice (e.g., Jesus setting the boundaries of ritual life and commerce by turning over the tables of moneychangers in the Temple in Matthew 21:12–13). Jesus' behavior does not reflect "perfection" with regard for the structures and rules of societal life; rather, Jesus' full connection to divine energy and clarity exemplifies uses of relational power to facilitate health and well-being. In each moment when Jesus held the upper hand in a relational dyad, he used his relational power appropriately. Consequently, Jesus never ab/used his relational power; he never sinned.

TRAUMATIZATION OF JESUS

While Jesus, the incarnate Christ, never abused his relational power, he did experience abuses of relational power that were traumatic. Every spring Christian churches honor through ritual remembrance and narrative re-telling Jesus' experiences of betrayal, unjust incarceration, bodily assault and violation, crucifixion, abandonment, death, and resurrection. The liturgical tradition names the period from Jesus' final gathering and meal with his disciples through the Saturday of lament Triduum. These three days, deemed "good" and "holy," reflect in the starkest terms the experience of traumatic abandonment, violation, and the liminal space of traumatic response.

Jesus was deemed a threat to the societal power of the religious and civil leadership in his society. Those holding significant economic, political, and religious social power arranged to offer money to one of Jesus' close associates and friends to betray their friendship and identify Jesus to authorities of the state who were then instructed to incarcerate Jesus without substantial cause. Out of fear, his friends and followers abandoned him and denied any association with him. Jesus endured unjust incarceration and questioning with testimony from those "bearing false witness." Following the pretense of a trial that functioned more as a form of social humiliation and performance of the power of civil authority in which Jesus was given the death penalty, Jesus was mocked and physically assaulted by officers of the state. Jesus was then publically and tortuously executed. During the hours in which he suffered, Jesus cried out his experience of being cut off from the relational connections of divine energy that had been central to his existence in incarnation and within the optimal relationality of the trinity. Abandoned and forsaken by the Trinitarian family, Jesus cries out the lamentation of Psalm 22. Unable to endure the traumatization and affliction of bodily, psychological, and relational wounding,[7] Jesus dies and his community flees in shame and fear on that "good" Friday.

At the very epicenter of Christian faith, community, and practice, stands the utter traumatization of Jesus, the Christ. To name the betrayal, crucifixion, and death of Jesus as anything but traumatic murder undermines the violence and tragedy of the event. Jesus did not survive his experiences of traumatic overwhelm and violence. His community hid in an upper room in terror. The women who loved him wept and held vigil at

7. Soelle, *Suffering*.

his burial site with secondary traumatization. And, traumatic loss entered into the community of the imminent trinity. The Friday of Jesus' death and the Saturday of traumatic paralyzation were horrifying to those living the darkness of the experience. They did not enjoy the benefit of knowing what would come. For those who loved and followed Jesus, the three days of betrayal, crucifixion, and existential uncertainty loomed large and heavy without sign or hope for reprieve.

Remaining present to the trauma of Jesus' murder and loss is challenging. It is no wonder why our religious communities are so quick to move on to the day of resurrection and restoration. Sitting vigil in the heart of the darkness brings us face to face with the most difficult of our human experiences. Yet, this liminal space, the betwixt and between of traumatic experience and response, offers us a powerful resource for the care of trauma. When we can abide in and remain present to the realities of traumatic experience and response, we open a space of authentic compassion and care for the parts, individuals, and communities among us who viscerally know the pain of traumatic violation. Authentically honoring the emotional space of traumatic experience and response within our sacred texts and communities of faith provide companionship to those living through traumatic response.

The "good news" offered in holding open the pain of these liturgical days as experienced by Jesus and those who love him rather than as a precursor to resolution and celebration is the offer of attuned and courageous connection during experiences of disconnection. It is the offer that you are not alone even in the midst of traumatic overwhelm, wounding, and disorientation. The primary traumatization that Jesus and the imminent trinity experienced really mattered. It wasn't just a scene in a larger orchestrated cosmic performance of divine power and triumph. The pain, violation, and disconnection of the crucifixion is reflected in the feelings of violation and isolation that accompany our experience of acute trauma and consequences of the accumulation of chronic, systemic abuses of power. The secondary traumatization and survival fear of the family and community of Jesus mattered and can function as a mirror of resonance for our own traumatized communities when we can tolerate holding and being present to, with, and/ or in the emotional space. When we quickly move towards the celebration of what is to come which remains unknown to those living through that Friday and Saturday, we diminish the full impact of traumatic disruption and risk adding to the feelings of isolation and abandonment. Let us honor the full experience of traumatic loss so that our sacred narratives and rituals may offer the balm of resonant connections even in the midst of our most painful experiences of disconnection and disruption.

Correspondingly, let us also resist the equivocation to be "like Jesus" if what it means to follow Jesus is to willingly submit to violations of bodily integrity and traumatic loss and wounding. Suffering, affliction, or trauma are not requirements for living a life of faith and pervert the desire of divine energy towards well-being and care. When those in power seek to abuse their relational power to harm or gratify their own desires without consent, the violations imposed on victim/survivors are not salvific, pedagogical, or the desire of God. Traumatic wounding does not save us. It is not an indicator of faithfulness, piety, or holiness. It does not honor God or divine energy or intention in the created world. Just as the traumatic death of Jesus grieved God, traumatic wounding of all those connected to the divine through the loving and vivifying energy of life grieves God. When we choose to abuse our relational power, we not only harm the subject of violation; we also dishonor and wound the source of life and connection of Self, God.

7

Restoring Connection

The darkness of traumatic experience/s can threaten to overwhelm all levels of our connectedness. Just as the Synoptic Gospel writers describe darkness covering the earth with the dying breath of Jesus, the darkness of traumatic wounding and sin can feel all pervasive with no end in sight. When we sin and abuse our relational power of care and responsibility towards the Earth and its non-human inhabitants, the ecological connections that keep the created order in order grow imbalanced and we begin to lose species and climatological sustainability. When we sin and abuse our relational power of social engagement and justice, we increasingly foster social systems that benefit the few and systemically oppress any communities who do not wield civil, economic, and/or legal power. The rules that govern our society grow in their brutalization of those with limited social power while greasing the wheels of success and wealth for those who have the power to influence. When we sin and abuse our relational power via relational dyads, we strain the bonds of loving connection and risk wounding and alienating those with whom we are in contact. When we sin and abuse our relational power internally, we further hurt parts of us that are already exiled and press our protective parts into more extreme and polarized strategies. And, when we sin and abuse our relational power against parts of self and all others, we wound the source of divine energy who flows through every entity and living organism in creation. The intrapersonal, interpersonal, societal, ecological, and spiritual connections that support and sustain all life are omnipresent; however, the wounding of experiencing and committing abuses of relational power have the capacity to weaken, disrupt, or eclipse the conduits of free, unbound, attuned, divine energy.

SIN AND THE ECLIPSING OF DIVINE CONNECTIONS

The connections to divine free energy may be disrupted, weakened, or eclipsed as parts of us disconnect and isolate in an effort to protect Self, the internal place of connection between the person and divine energy, from the wounds of sin. Sin, as the abuses of relational power, initiates protective strategies within and among persons to protect from further wounding. These processes are initiated when we are sinned against and when we perpetrate sin. If the processes of protection remain dominant, they become reinforced and we begin to organize life around the wounds of sins and disruptions to our source of life and resiliency become our relational norms. The commission and violations of sin both shift human beings into parts-dominated systems of protection and away from being a Self-led internal and relational system of attuned connection and gracious wisdom.

When we are sinned against, with or without traumatic overwhelm and accompanying traumatic response, parts of us receive the wounding and beliefs about self and the world that emerge from the injury. These parts take the proverbial bullet in an effort to protect Self and then often are scapegoated or exiled by other parts of the psycho-spiritual-somatic system of the individual. If the offense is subjectively minimal enough, the degree of exilation or internal disconnection is also minimal. If the wound is subjectively experienced as an existential threat, the degree of internal disconnection is nearly complete. The consequence of a part altruistically receiving the burden of the wounds of sin in order to protect Self is that the wounded part now carries the content of the threat and is then perceived as a threat by the other parts of the system. These other parts then begin to organize themselves and take on roles within the system to protect the part that is wounded and to protect our awareness and felt sense from the emotions, sensations, beliefs, and/or memories of the wounded part. This reorganization occurs along a continuum and with the intention of continuing to protect Self from sin. Unfortunately, the consequence of the protective inclinations and strategies employed by parts rather than Self is increasing disconnection from the divine connecting energy through Self. The connections to and of divine free energy do not diminish or disappear; rather, they can get covered over in an effort to protect the connections from the wounding of experiences of sin.

Likewise, commissions of sin often are a consequence of an imbalanced system seeking to overcompensate for prior experiences of harm. In other words, we sin in a misguided attempt to protect our system from experiencing again the wounds of being sinned against. Protective parts take on increasingly rigid and extreme strategies for obtaining and maintaining social power to reduce the likelihood of feeling vulnerable and overwhelmed again. This pattern of increasing parts-led strategies of protection is visible when the child who is abused at home becomes the playground bully, the community who has endured centuries of violence and oppression seeks a variety of means to numb out the internal rage that is unsafe to express and threatens to overwhelm, the nation who commits genocide as a means of reestablishing national pride following humiliation, or the survivors of genocide who establish a new nation and then protect that nation by committing atrocities towards their neighbor. Experiences of being on the receiving end of sin and wounding, traumatic or non-traumatic, have the potential to foster increasingly parts-led systems. Parts-led systems are organized to protect; however, they often function from a place of fear that prompts ever expanding strategies of isolation and disconnection from the source of creativity, vitality, and authentic and fulfilling life.

Commissions of sin that increase disconnection to divine energy also occur when we are living within a social structure that limits choice. This phenomena is most vividly, though not exclusively, witnessed in the distress experienced by military personnel who, in following orders to advance the mission or protect fellow soldiers, perform behaviors that go against their moral code. Recently, the term "moral injury"[1] has been utilized to describe the trauma-like responses observed in military personnel as a consequence of their actions that inflicted traumatic wounding on others. "Moral injury results when soldiers violate their core moral beliefs, and in evaluating their behavior negatively, they feel they no longer live in a reliable, meaningful world and can no longer be regarded as decent human beings. They may feel this even if what they did was warranted and unavoidable . . . Seeing someone else violate core moral values or feeling betrayed by persons in authority can also lead to a loss of meaning and faith."[2] While Brock and Lettini are clear to point out that moral injury differs from PTSD, specifically with regard to the physiological dimensions of traumatic response, they do illuminate the significant distress of experiencing the eclipse of divine presence and energy and rise of extreme protective and escape oriented parts

---

1. Rita Nakashima Brock and Gabriella Lettini have led the way in theological reflection on moral injury. See Brock and Lettini, *Soul Repair* and Soul-Repair Center at Brite Divinity School.

2. Ibid., xv.

in the face of experiencing and coping with moral injury. The behavioral consequences of moral injury include many of the extreme strategies parts employ when keeping traumatized exiles at bay, including manager parts who become rigid and controlling or firefighter/escape artist parts who utilize drugs, alcohol, rage, or suicide to escape the pain of moral injury. While research on moral injury is currently focused on the experiences of military personnel, I also wonder about its relevancy for those whose life experiences and choices are significantly limited by structures of sin and oppression that intentionally or unintentionally pit survival against morality, including the limitation imposed by incarceration, poverty, or domestic oppression.

When we are the party who abuses relational power and commits sin against others, whether out of our need to protect against additional experiences of being wounded or through adherence to the directives of others in power over us, we experience a decrease in our capacity to access Self energy and divine connection. In parallel to the processes of protection that lead toward disconnection in favor of perceived control, the commissions of relational abuses, whether out of wounding or systems of constraint, also move our internal systems into positions of parts-led rigidity or escape and away from the healthy vulnerability that accompanies divine connections and Self leadership of our internal parts. Divine connection through Self remains ever present and always available to resume trust, attachment, and loving direction. Divine presence and connection is not shattered or annihilated by the commission or experiencing of sin; it always remains ever present. We all intuitively know how precious the energy of divine presence and connection is to our life and our parts will do anything in their power to protect this connection even to the extent of walling it off from our awareness.

Life is all about connections to and of free, unbound, fluid, life-granting, life-sustaining energy. The connections of divine energy hold us together within ourselves, in relationship with others, in community, and with God. While trauma and sin disrupt connections leading to extreme responses among the various parts within our being, they do not have to retain unhealthy strategies of protection that keep divine presence locked "safely" away. Reestablishing connection to the flow of divine free energy through Self and coursing through all entities and organisms in the world is always available. It is not a matter of generating connections; it is about helping parts within each person, segments of communities, and dimensions of ecological webs to ease up and relax the fears that fuel now maladaptive protective strategies. Connection within, among, and to God and divine energy in all is always available and reconnection is the key to resiliency from the wounds of sin. As we become more capable of allowing ourselves to connect to the vivifying energy of life, we also become more capable of fostering relationships of care, authenticity, and equitable uses of relational power. As we allow the barrier of sin that eclipses our access to divine free energy and connection to pass, we become ever more aware of the grace of compassion, curiosity, courage, clarity, calmness, creativity, confidence, groundedness, and connection among all the parts of our internal and external relational systems.

THE SEARCH FOR WHAT SAVES: A SOTERIOLOGY

Restoration of the flow of divine energy through life and relationships is the source of a life of authentic, attuned, compassionate wisdom. It is what saves us from the disconnections that result from sin leaving communities in disarray and individuals isolated from loving awareness of the whole of who we are and contributing to the felt sense of separation from God and the global web of life. The theological term "salvation" is etymologically derived from *salvus,* or, healed. Salvation, ultimately, is about healing, soothing, and unburdening the wounds and beliefs consequent to sinful abuses of relational power, including those that reach the degree of traumatic overwhelm and those that remain below that threshold.

While Christian interpretations of "salvation" have varied over the history of the church, the question of what saves us theologically is directly linked to our understanding and confession of the nature and character of sin. If the problem of humanity is pride, then the solution is humility. If the human illness is ignorance, then the remedy is knowledge. If human sin is the rejection of the authority and power of God, then salvation is submission to God. For example, in the early Greek church, salvation was the escape from death and error; for the Roman Catholics, it is need to escape guilt and its immediate and eternal consequences; for the classical Protestant, salvation is resolution from the anxiety producing law; and for traditions of Pietism, it is transformation from a godless existence through conversion and becoming born again.[3] The dominant language and images used to describe and name sin and salvation are important because how

3. Tillich, *Systematic Theology,* vol 2, 166.

we understand and frame the problem directly influences the available and effective solutions. For trauma-sensitive theology, sin is the abuses of relational power that cause disruptions in the flow of divine energy and presence. Consequently, salvation includes healing the wounds caused by sin and reestablishing right and attuned relationships through the restoration of our connection to the divine energy and presence within each organism.

Reorienting our understanding of salvation towards a desire for healing is immensely helpful for trauma-sensitive theology and praxis. Paul Tillich discussed sin as the problem of being estranged from our authentic being or the experience of being parts led without connection to Self. He writes, "Salvation as "healing" "corresponds to the state of estrangement as the main characteristic of existence. In this sense, healing means reuniting with that which is estranged, giving a center to what is split, overcoming the split between God and [hu]man, [hu]man and [their] world, [hu]man and self . . . Salvation is reclaiming from the old and transferring into the New Being."[4] Tillich offers the image of Christ as the New Being as "the undistorted manifestation of essential being within and under the conditions of existence."[5] Translated into the language of trauma-sensitive theology, Christ, the New Being, is fully connected, unburdened, and the Self-led promised hope of humanity existence. Salvation or healing, with an interpretation of Tillich, includes welcoming home the parts of self and community who have been estranged and exiled, overcoming the internal tug-of-war as protective systems vie for control in how to negotiate the world, cultivating trust in the internal Self that is available to hold with care and love all parts, and moving towards an internal and external life characterized by relationality of compassionate, courageous connection with the divine, the web of life, and external and internal community.

The process of salvation is the restoration of connections to divine presence and energy that facilitate the healing of wounds and releasing the burdens resulting from the sins of abuses of relational power. The theological choice to portray the path of salvation as ongoing or as something that is accomplished in a single moment by the death/resurrection of Jesus or with the performance of a single religious ritual like baptism or confirmation reflects the larger systematic framework being utilized. Within the framework of Christian theology, what saves us is traditionally linked to

4. Ibid. Alterations made to change "man" to "human" to reflect connections to persons of all genders.

5. Ibid., 119.

the person and work of Jesus, the Christ. How does the incarnation of Jesus and embodiment of the second person of the imminent trinity contribute to the reestablishment of connection between God and humanity? How does Jesus impact the prevalence and consequence of sin? The way in which one answers these questions sets the trajectory of soteriology and the forms of relationality that are included in the path of salvation. Trauma-sensitive theology, along with other constructive models of theology including Tillich, acknowledges at least three levels of relationality in need of care and reconnection. The relationship between God and humanity, among and within human communities, and between the Self and parts of each person. Reconnection of relationship between God and humanity traditionally falls under the purview of theories of atonement, or at-one-ment.

Options for Atonement

Historically, there have been three predominant theories to explain the significance and function of the presence of Jesus as the intermediary between God and creation, or the means of atonement. While there are more than three options available, the most common and widely preached and taught atonement theories are Anselm's satisfaction theory, the ransom theory originally credited Origin with a revision by Aulen, and Abelard's moral influence theory. Remembering that all theological categories are linked together in order to paint a cohesive image and narrative of how the world functions, God's role and power in the world, aspirations of creation, fundamental nature of human beings, presence and detriment of sin, particularity of the incarnate Christ, hope of salvation, role and function of the Holy Spirit, gathering of the community, promise of completion, and ethics for right living, it is to be of no surprise that the traditional theological options of atonement also reflect the larger theological themes and concerns that undergird theological formation.

Perhaps the single most influential atonement theory is Anselm's satisfaction model. This option is summed up in the oft confessed idea that Jesus had to die on the cross to pay the debt of sin that human beings owed but could not pay to God. God's righteous anger towards the disobedience and pride of humanity demanded satisfaction or payment for wrong doing. In this model, God's power is absolute, creation is a disappointment, human beings are inherently flawed and sinful, sin is prideful disobedience to the authority and honor of God, Jesus is the flawless payment that is the sole option for easing the indignation of God, atonement/at-one-ment with God is achieved through Jesus' death payment on the cross, and the life of Jesus counts primarily as evidence of his innocence and worthiness to pay the debt of honor. While preached with regularity on any given Sunday, this model has the potential to do as much harm as good through its reinforcement of divine power and portrayal of God as demanding of human sacrifice as the means of restitution for the offense of dishonor. It does not take too much imagination to see how this model could embolden traumatizing abuses of relational power when merged with domestic models of male power.

The christus victor atonement model describes the world as the scene of a cosmic battle between the forces of good led by God and powers of evil led by the devil. Human beings are the primary site of the battle as each side works through human beings to enact benevolence or violence. Due to humanity's predisposition towards sin, the forces of evil threaten to have the upper hand. God sent Jesus to live among humanity as a spiritual Trojan horse. The devil took the bait in having the forces of evil crucify Jesus. Jesus descended in Hell and defeated the devil, becoming the victorious Christ. While humanity continues to struggle with the sins of violence and pride due to the remaining spirits of evil that continue to engage in spiritual warfare, the ultimate battle is won due to the actions of Jesus. As human beings continue to live in community and the world, the "fruits of the Spirit" serve as an indication of whose side of the cosmic battle an individual is on. Those who dress themselves in the "armor of God"[6] and seek to serve God's forces of good are identified as holy and warriors of God. The underlying challenge issued by this model is the necessity of strife and opposition. The model hinges on an understanding of power as domination and victory in a cosmic us versus them binary. There is little space for multiplicity or complexity in an at-*one*-ment model that requires ultimate domination of one over another.

The third most common model of atonement is Abelard's moral influence theory. Unlike the previous models that place the bulk of the significance of Jesus in the work of his death, the moral influence theory emphasizes the life of Jesus. Human beings are separated from God and one another through sin as a loss of moral integrity. Because God desires reunification, God offered human beings natural law, ritual law, and social law in

---

6. A reference to Ephesians 6:10–18 that is popular among those who adhere to a christus victor model of atonement and salvation.

an effort to induce moral living but the law itself was not effective enough to restore moral living to humanity. Jesus was sent as an example of how to live a moral life that is pleasing to God and in harmony with the created order. The life of Jesus is a model exemplar of how to live in harmony and the death of Jesus is intended to impress humanity with the depth of Jesus' love and inspire others to follow in his example. Distinct from the other two options, the moral influence theory is more about human disposition and behavior and less about justifying the needs of God. The shift in focus from appeasing God's honor or assisting in God's victory over the devil to the character of human beings in the aim of living a moral life alters the intended audience of the death of Jesus. "For Abelard, the problem of atonement was not how to change an offended God's mind toward the sinner, but how to bring sinful humankind to see that the God they perceived as harsh and judgmental was actually loving. Thus for Abelard, Jesus died as the demonstration of God's love. And the change that results from that loving death is not in God but in the subjective consciousness of the sinners, who repent and cease their rebellion against God and turn towards God."[7] Salvation is possible through changes in the subjective being of humanity. The limitation of the moral influence theory is in the absence of how human beings overcome the consequences of amorality or sin in order to authentically live the moral life rather than perform the moral life.

Atonement Theologies and the Valorization of Trauma and Death

Despite their unique distinctions, all of the most prevalent atonement theories share a common problem: God's sending Jesus into human history with the primary purpose of death. While the rationale for Jesus' death varies, the suffering, traumatic death of Jesus remains a central feature of these soteriologies. Theologies that valorize the traumatization and execution of Jesus as the essential feature of salvation and divine revelation, either intentionally or unintentionally, promote the enduring of abusive suffering as the marks of a pious Christian life and are dangerous. They are dangerous in that they function to sacrilize enduring sinful abuses of power and reinforce social and interpersonal relationships that value harmful relational connections over healthy relational connections. Atonement theologies built around satiating God's righteous anger, spiritual warfare that bifurcates human community and severs connections, or traumatic death as a

7. Weaver, *The Nonviolent Atonement*.

signal of absolute love all risk contributing to abuses of relational power. Theological messages that emerge from these theologies include "bear your suffering as Jesus suffered for your sake," "God never gives us more than we can endure," "human beings are so sinful that God had to kill his own son in order to save you," or "God ordained this union so you must submit" and have functioned in the context of abuses of relational power (sin) to spiritualize traumatic suffering and keep victim/survivors within abusive relationships and discouraging them from seeking well-being. Theologies of salvific or pedagogical suffering reinforce suffering and traumatization and systems of relational power that trade the pleasure of one party for the well-being of the other thereby nearly eliminat the possibility of authentic, restorative connections and attachment.

The traumatizing death of Jesus is not in any way salvific or redemptive in and of itself. It is not a paradigm for holy sacrifice. Traumatic overwhelm, suffering, and death are not a means to a good. The benefit of the betrayal, crucifixion, and forsakenness Jesus experienced through his death is not universal salvation; rather, if there is any, it is the expansion of God's capacity for full understanding of the wounding and burden of trauma. The traumatizing death of Jesus, which included the betrayal trauma[8] of the experience of being forsaken by the first person of the Trinity in an effort to protect the source of divine energy in the world, introduced the full weight and burden of trauma into the subjective experience of God. The impact and threat of traumatic disruption reached into the depths of the imminent Trinity and, in a moment of shock, the full flow of divine life giving energy to Jesus ceased. In the midst of the darkness and void of Saturday, all waited with bated breath for signs of renewal of divine connection. What would be the response of loving, attuned, vivifying divine energy and presence to the brash and self righteous infliction of trauma and death for the primary purpose of protecting and reinforcing human systems of abusive power?

God's response to the evil of humanity's gross abuse of relational power towards Jesus is the potential for redemption and the promise of resurrection; the hopes for reconnection and healing the wounds that keep us in patterns of disconnection and rigid protection. Through the incarnation of the Christ as the embodied Jesus, God, as the optimally relational and fully connected imminent Trinity, welcomed the experience of internal distinctions, the slight separation within the imminent Trinity that must have occurred with the incarnation. The human experience of Jesus, the

---

8. Freyd and DePrince, *Trauma and Cognitive Science*.

Christ offered an opportunity for God to amplify the divine's felt sense and understanding of the existential experience of human beings. Prior to incarnation, the subjectivity of divine presence was with all existing entities and organisms; however, the connections were incomplete and mitigated due to the need of organisms to protect parts from harm. Through the incarnation, divine presence and energy was offered access to the full existential experience of humanity, unblocked and with the full trust and leadership of the connection between the divine and the Self of Jesus. While the life of Jesus demonstrated the potential of a life lived in harmony with divine presence, the traumatizing death of Jesus introduced the fullness of traumatic experience into the subjective awareness of the divine community. This awareness of trauma and death within the being of God generated a greater depth of empathy towards human struggle and prompting an increase in the presence of Spirit in the world.

For trauma-sensitive theology and praxis, the problem of sin is the abuse of relational power and the resulting wounding and burdens that lead to disruptions in internal, communal, and divine connections. Any atonement theology or soteriology that fails to confront violent abuses of power lacks the clarity and fortitude to honorably and authentically speak to the multidimensionality of contemporary life, self-awareness, and relationality. The doctrine of salvation within a constructive and systematic theology that seeks to be mindful of the prevalence and impact of traumatic wounding, response, and resiliency must include a means for the reestablishment and reinforcing of connections to the loving free energy of divine presence. Salvation doesn't require appeasing divine wrath, winning a cosmic war, or inducing through traumatizing death motivation for morality. Salvation requires healing of wounds, the unburdening of parts, and reconnection with the omnipresent loving energy of God. The life of Jesus, fulfilled without abusing relational power and utilizing power to protect the vulnerable ones in society, does provide a model of harmonious internal system fully led by the divine energy of Self free from disruption or eclipse.

Redemption and Resurrection as Healing Paths

Atonement between all of the created order and the divine is cultivated through empathetic connection and a fuller knowing of the trauma of existential wounding and sin within the being of God. The restoration of the relationship is not a matter of generating connection ex nihilo; it is a reclamation of the loving presence that always already is. The "work" of Jesus the incarnate Christ is to increase divine awareness of the subjective experience of life in a world that includes harm, disruption, and wounding. The incorporation of Jesus' experience of life lived with the fullness of divine connection and concluding in the traumatic dissolution of connection in crucifixion and death provides the means for an amplification of compassionate informed care in God's offer of loving presence and vivifying energy. Resolution of the disruption of connection between God and humanity is a free offering available to all. The *salvus* of interpersonal and intrapersonal connections are the work of each person through connection to the restorative capacity of divine connection.

What is the process through which human beings participate in the restoration of relational connections? Tillich offers and describes a "threefold character of salvation in which the effect of the divine atoning act upon [humanity] is expressed: participation, acceptance, transformation (in classical terminology, Regeneration, Justification, Sanctification)."[9] The lenses of participation, acceptance, and transformation are useful in the easing parts of self that feel overwhelmed or anxious about the process of reengagement with the divine, others, or parts who have caused pain in the attempt to protect. Simply stated, participation is the recognition of the presence of Self within. Reconnection of attuned attachments begin with a noticing of divine presence that has never left or abandoned us. Self energy and divine presence may have been eclipsed as a protective strategy during times of traumatic distress but it remains steadfast and available once life becomes "safe enough." Participation only requires the courage and curiosity to attend to the "still small voice" of wisdom and compassion within. Acceptance is the process of clearly acknowledging the ways in which each of us has endured sin, the ways in which we have perpetrated sin, and the impact of both experiences of sin on internal and external relationships. We cannot begin the process of change until we first acknowledge with clarity and courage the reality of what currently is. Acceptance necessitates an open welcoming of our own wounded and exiled parts in need of care and compassion and the parts of us who have perpetrated abuses of power out of a need to protect or from a place of fear. The paths of acceptance and care differ for the parts that are wounded by experiences of being sinned against and those who committed sin. Transformation is the process of unburdening and the restoration of parts to their true and authentic being

9. Tillich, *Systematic Theology*, vol. 2, 176.

prior to wounding. Full transformation is witnessed in the resurrected Jesus. While full and complete unburdening and transformation is challenged through life in a relational world that continues to be marked by abuses of relational power, it is possible, with attention, intention, and care, to begin the journey of unburdening and transformative healing of internal wounds and generate ever increasing Self-led relationships.

Participation in divine energy and presence is the birthright given to all living organisms through the presence of God and attachment of the divine to the centered Self. Acceptance requires more attention in this space due to the complexities of translating theological language into the felt sense of lived experience. We are all clear of the ways in which we experience the wounding of being sinned against as distinct from the feelings of perpetrating sin; however, most of our theological systems fail to adequately account for the difference when naming sin and doctrines of "redemption." Theologically, the term "redemption" is most often related to the need of sinful humanity to be "bought back" from the evil one either through the victory of Jesus in christus victor or the debt owed to the honor of God in satisfaction theory. In either case, the consequence of sin, however it is defined in the particular theological system, is separation from God that requires a payment for reunification. At its most fundamental description, "redemption" models are derived from economics where payment grants access. Traditional atonement theories, like those described in the previous section, hold that human beings are incapable of offering adequate payment due to their sin and require Jesus to pay on our behalf. These models are helpful in highlighting the disruptions of relationality caused by sin and abuses of relational power as well as the need to make restitution for the harms we are responsible for causing. Those of us with enough internal connections to Self and awareness of the pain generated through the wounding of parts carry burdens associated with the harms we have perpetrated. The burdens of guilt related to our perpetration of abuses of relational power can either prompt a greater cultivation of empathy or calcify into an additional strategy of protection and defense. The more recalcitrant our systems become in protecting us from our original exiled wounds though ever expanding strategies of defense reducing our awareness of our own pain and the pain we inflict on others, the more likely we are to continue to violate boundaries and abuse our relational power. The hope of redemption is the potential for restoration of connection to divine energy through the relaxation of protective parts and fostering of trust between protective and wounded parts through Self. God has already equipped every living organism with the means of restoring connection. The task of redemption falls to each of us in caring for the burdens that accrue when we violate the boundaries of others and turn towards parts fears and strategies and away from our internal, intrinsic connections to divine presence.

Each of us requires redemption for the ways in which we have abused our relational power; but what about the wounds that we carry from experiences of being sinned against? Utilizing the theological language of redemption in reference to experiences of traumatic wounding due to abuses of relational power either by social institutions, other persons, or parts of oneself unnecessarily conflates parts that hold guilt from commissions of sin and those that hold shame from experiencing the wounding of sin. Too often, survivors of traumatic events unnecessarily accept responsibility for the actions of others as a means of coping with the sensations and emotions of overwhelm and helplessness. Accepting responsibility for the harmful actions of another affords the appearance of control; however, the appearance of control demands a stiff price: guilt, shame, and internalization and acceptance of the sin of another. Redemption language, when used in connection with trauma, is an inappropriate appropriation of the concept of redemption because it assigns responsibility to the wrong party. Victim/survivors of trauma do not require the redemption of their experience as if they were responsible for the violation of relational boundaries. Those responsible for committing violence and traumatizing another must be held responsible for their sinful actions and require redemption. The category of redemption, when applied to survivors of traumatic experience, unintentionally reinforces the trauma by perpetuating a tendency of blaming the victim by misappropriating the "sin."

Reconnection to divine energy and fullness of life for the species, communities, individuals, or parts of us who have been wounded and burdened by the sins of others requires a different theological lens. For Jesus, who embodies only the wounds of being sinned against and none of the burdens of perpetrating sin, we solely utilize the language of resurrection. Because Jesus was without sin, he did not need redemption. Rather, God demonstrated the gift of the full reestablishment of unconstrained divine connection through the resurrection of Jesus. Jesus is resurrected as a response to traumatic death without abuse of relational power or sin and provides a lens for how to theologically reflect on the wounds and burdens generated by being sinned against. Resurrection goes a step further than redemption in offering the full reestablishing of connections of divine energy within and among all parts and beings. It offers a theological model for the hope of the full unburdening of all the various parts that carry wounds and no longer functional beliefs. Resurrection carries the promise of healing the wounds of all parts and offers a path for the journey towards increasing experiences of Self leadership with attunement and fuller connection to divine free energy. Resurrection is the promise of transformation and the completion of restoring full connection.

Redemption of sins committed and resurrection of the body sinned against are God's divine answer to the traumatic disruptions of relationship and connection. Just as Jesus, the one who lived in fullness of Self leadership and without sin, was restored via resurrection, there is always the potential for resiliency and resurrection of the exiled parts within and among us. Resurrection, while marking the complete re/membering of divine connection to loving free energy of God, is not a wholesale return to the "before." The scars marking the experiences of trauma remain not as a haunting presence of traumatic response but as a testimony and witness of the strength of survival and the tenacity of resiliency and love. The priority of bodily experience and the need for full acceptance of trauma narratives, two of the four primary commitments of trauma-sensitive theology, are reflected in the body of the resurrected Jesus. The scars of traumatic wounding remain on his hands and body as testimony to this experience of trauma and death. They function as a means of identification as well as a symbol of the capacity for recovery and the healing over without erasure of wounds.

Resurrection and, in time, ascension are divine response to the traumatic death of Jesus and make possible the joyous, full reunion of all persons of the imminent Trinity. Through the full restoration of relational connections to the source of divine presence and energy, Jesus was able to fully unburden and heal the wounds of traumatic abuses of power and return to Self leadership with unfettered communion with all. The promise and hope of resurrection offers opportunity for relational restoration of earthly relationality, emboldens courage, and soothes the secondary traumatization of loved ones. During the time following resurrection, Jesus abided with his community and offered respite from fear, confusion, and exaggerated protective responses. The physical presence and communion Jesus, the incarnate Christ, offers his community, in the most visible and tangible way, the hope of renewed connections that can soothe the pain of loss, fear, and trauma of all forms. The resurrection and ascension of Jesus reveal the desire of God for full restoration of connections of divine energy and relationality. For human beings, full restoration requires redemption of the parts of us who participate in abuses of relational power as well as resurrection of the hurting and exiled parts of us wounded by sin. When all parts are released from the constraints of sin, via commission or reception, we are more fully available to the wisdom of divine presence through the connection and influence of the Spirit and enter into more authentic and fulfilling intra- and interpersonal communion.

8

Enriching Attunement

Reestablishing connections to divine energy through Self, offering those avenues of care to wounded and protective internal parts, and extending the grace of healthy relationality to others outside our embodied being is the journey towards a fulfilled, authentic, balanced, and harmonious life and world. The original grace of the gift of divine free energy that attaches all that lives and moves and has its being to the source of all life and the promise of the hope of salvific healing flows from the invitational power of God. The power of the divine presence and intention beckons each of us towards fullness of life through the attuned care of all parts of our own embodied being, community, and the full ecological web of life. The restoration of connection offered through the redemption of the wounds of sins committed and resurrection of our exiled or traumatized parts provides space for the cultivation of care and love for all parts of who we are, grace for those with whom we live in community, and an ever deepening and expanding sense of the flow of living energy and love that connects all. Growing in awareness of the presence of divine energy is not a given within existence. There are many persons who live their lives under the cloak of their protective parts with only rare glimpses of the depth of relationality available. Experiences of relational wounding and trauma do have a profound impact on our ability to trust Self, others, and God; however, because of the experiences of the incarnate, fully embodied Jesus the disconnections due to traumatic overwhelm do not have the last word. The wounds of trauma can be eased, connections can be restored, and resonance with divine energy can be enriched, attuned, and utilized as a resource for fullness of life. Once we begin the journey of reestablishing connections within our own internal system of parts, with others, and God, we then begin the second task of attuning and enhancing our re-established connections.

Attunement, according to the *Oxford English Dictionary*, is the "bringing into harmony" and is etymologically connected to "attune' (tuneful accord or harmony) as well as 'atone' (agreement, reconciliation)."[1] Attunement is the process of increasing in alignment with another and can be a rich resource of cultivating empathy, resonance, and compassionate awareness. It is the intention of "tuning in" with increasing clarity and resonance. The practice of attuning to God, self, or others requires a cultivation of patience, somatic awareness, and a resting into moments of stillness. Attuning to the quality of Self energy within often means directing our attention inward so that we can begin to notice the distinctive senses or frequencies of various parts and the space of peaceful, compassionate groundedness that resides at the most fundamental expression of our being. Attuning to others is most successfully possible once we have attuned to Self and our own parts. When we can notice the various qualities of affect and energy within, we are better equipped to distinguish our resonance with another's affect or parts as distinct from our own and extend the care we give to our internal parts to the parts of another. This process is a gift and skill. It requires us to "tune-in" and resist the cultural pull of "tuning out."

All of these components of attunement run directly counter to the pace and aims of contemporary society that values ephemeral entertainment, immediate satisfaction, and disconnection. We are regularly bombard by messages that amplify the insecurities and fears of our wounded parts. The bulk of the marketing industry depends on the woundedness of our parts to sell us security systems for our homes, dieting and exercise programs to mold our bodies, beauty products to meet culturally dependent and ever shifting markers of beauty. Likewise, our current addictions to social media updates, constant dropping of news stories, and immediate access to communication requests via text messages or social media engagements fuel a pace and quality of interaction that is rapid, short-lived, and lacks the elements of connection that have the capacity to sustain and enrich our connections and attunement. Resonant of Augustine's confession,[2] our hearts and beings are continually restless and struggle to settle into the very practices that can offer respite and reprieve. We crave intimate attachments of empathetic attunement; yet, in the desperation of our search we over-

1. Lipari, *Listening, Thinking, Being*, 206.
2. "Our hearts are restless until they find rest in thee." Augustine, *Confessions*.

look the still and quiet resources we seek. Attuning to the gentle, sturdy, compassionate presence of God requires trust in abiding grace, safety in vulnerability, and a willingness to attend to the stillness and softness of somatic wisdom. These qualities have the power to counter dimensions of our culture that offer fads instead of the practices of somatic wisdom, cultivation of intuition, and fuller knowing of all dimensions of self that truly sustain us. The wisdom offered through somatic awareness, development of our capacity to experience and trust our intuition, and the resources of healing our internal systems come from our connection to divine Spirit. Enhancing our attunement to the presence of divine energy in the world and in our lives is fostered through our connection to the Spirit of the fullness of life, the third person of the Trinity.

SPIRIT OF FULLNESS OF LIFE: A PNEUMATOLOGY

The power of attuned, resonant attachments among parts and between beings harkens us back to two powerful images of beginnings in the Christian sacred texts: first, the narratives of the beginning of matter and form that create the world we know; second, the beginning of the expansion of Christian community on the day of Pentecost in Acts. In both tales of beginnings, the Spirit is present and formative in calling forth and vivifying a newness of life and being through the first community of living beings and the second community of faith in the promise of the resurrected one.

As you recall, "*When* Elohim *began to create the heaven and the earth—(2) the earth was* tohu va bohu ("waste and wild") *and darkness was upon the face of* tehom ("oceanic deep") *and* ruach ("Spirit") *was pulsing over the face of the waters—(3) then* Elohim *said let there be light . . .*"[3] At the beginning and in the presence of the waste and wild of the dark oceanic deep, Spirit pulsed or vibrated over the watery chaos of matter and energy. Even in these opening, invocating lines, the Spirit is present, hovering, pulsing, resonating, attuning with the energy and matter of creation as Elohim crafted the energy of the deep into the frequencies of light. If we frame Elohim as the agent of binding the energy into matter, form, and light, Spirit is the ever abiding companion who was and is "with." Spirit is present with the elemental and watery chaos before it becomes. The grace of the loving presence offered to creation by Spirit before formation is exquisite. It is fully attuned, resonant, and accepting of the rawness of begin-

3. Translation from Keller, *On the Mystery*, 48. See also Keller, *Face of the Deep.*

ning matter even before creation is pronounced "good." The profound gift of the Spirit's presence is the revelation of the gracious and loving capacity of the Spirit to be fully present to the chaos and "mess" of elemental matter at the beginning and within each of us, and to meet us with full acceptance and positive regard. The abiding, attuned presence of Spirit is integral in the quality of the formation of the elemental, watery, chaos. Spirit doesn't require anything from the tohu va bohu or tehom other than its being.

In addition to the quality of abiding, resonant attunement invoked in the Priestly account, "Spirit," through its linguistic roots in the Semitic and Indo-Germanic languages, is also deeply connected to "breath."[4] The flow of air coursing over the face of the earth and infusing our bodies with every inhale and exhale beautifully mirrors the pulsing of ruach over the face of the waters. Breath, for many cultures, is the paradigmatic symbol of life. This connection of body, breath, earth, and life emerges in our religious and cultural consciousness in the image of God carefully and lovingly crafting the human from the humus and breathing into the human's body "the breath of life; and the human became a living being" (Gen 2:7 NRSV). The rhythmic, undulating flow of breath is one of the few body processes that is under both conscious and unconscious control, giving us the option of either attending to the quality and flow of breath or focusing on other dimensions of life. Whether we pay attention to our breath or trust it to continue without reflection, our breath of life connects us to the abundance of our external world from our first breath to our last. Attending to our breath can be a powerful resource in helping us attune to divine presence and action in the world, to our own internal parts and being, and to resonate with the energy and flow of Spirit within others while maintaining our sense of stability and grounding. Spirit as holy presence and the breath of life provides an evocative and vibrant image of the work of the third person of the imminent Trinity in the world as abundant resource, omnipresence, flowing, enlivening grace, and conduit of vitality and rich connection to God, self, others, and the world.

The images of Spirit as pulsating, vibrating, resonant energy and as flowing, life giving, abundant breath in the creation narratives at the beginnings of our sacred texts invite us to imagine Spirit as intimately infused with and integral to the creation and sustaining of all dimensions of life and living beings. As contrast to the doctrine of *creatio ex nihilo*, creation from nothing, a theology of Spirit as fullness of life invokes a theology of *creatio*

---

4. Tillich, *Systematic Theology,* vol. 3, 21.

ex profundus, creation from the depths, and *creatio continua*, creation as continuing creativity and generativity. The creative energy and presence of Spirit honors the depths of what already is without limiting the potential of what can be. The dual care towards the depths along with visions and hopes of what can emerge are essential to the work of the Spirit and the care of wounded souls and parts. The emergence, growth, fulfillment, and deterioration of living organisms is an ongoing feature of creation and the creative expression of human beings and culture.

Life is dynamic and flows along established rhythms and guides that wed together the "from" of structures needed for life to flourish with the "for" of freedom for novelty and emergence. The structures of life range from the double helix of our DNA to the cultural forms we enact to order society. Often times, the structures of life are experienced in terms of the limitations they impose. We get frustrated by our inability to engage with full freedom and ability either through the limits of our context or the limits of our biological ability. On the other hand, structures and boundaries can also free us to move towards our fullest selves. Maintaining the potential of all possibilities paralyzes more often than it motivates. Our potential to participate in the ongoing creative work of the Spirit directs us towards working with what is present in our midst and available to us. The freedom of novelty and emergence works with what is present. Rather than becoming lost in the "coulds" and "shoulds," creative and generative participation in the work of the Spirit in our lives and worlds honors the gift of what is present and imagines this gift in its fullest expression. This balance of structure and freedom guides our natural and cultural worlds as we accept with grace "from" what is and imagine continuation of what can be. With a specific eye toward the role of human beings in the cultivation and crafting of our cultural and, ever increasingly, natural worlds, Philip Hefner's term "created co-creators" aptly honors and directs the role of the involvement of human agents in the ongoing creative work of the Spirit.[5] As human beings expand our capacity to impact our global environment for good or harm, we also have a responsibility to commune with the Spirit who dwells within us in order to remain a beneficent partner in the creative flow of the Spirit.

The Spirit who pulses over the deep and breathes life into creation continues in active participation with humanity in the formation of vibrant and healthy communities—which returns us to our second narrative of Spirit-led beginnings. After the resurrection and ascension of Jesus, Luke/

5. Hefner, *The Human Factor*.

Acts recounts the story of the community of Jesus gathered together for prayer with eager expectation and hope of receiving the gift or promise of the "baptism of the Holy Spirit" (Acts 1:5 NRSV). The image of baptism signifies a quality of washing, covering over, immersing and is a symbol of community affiliation and inclusion. What could those early follow-ers of Jesus have anticipated when he instructed them to stay in the area? Whatever they hoped for and imagined was far surpassed. On the day of Pentecost, the Spirit of the fullness of life enveloped each of those present and they experienced the depth of divine presence and connection that transcended the boundaries of language, culture, and fear and wounding. Acts recounts,

> When the day of Pentecost had come, they were all together in one place. And suddenly from heaven there came a sound like the rush of a violent wind, and it filled the entire house where they were sitting. Divided tongues, as of fire, appeared among them, and a tongue rested on each of them. All of them were filled with the Holy Spirit and began to speak in other languages, as the Spirit gave them ability. (Acts 2:1–5 NRSV)

The presence of divine Spirit rushed through the community, immediately transforming them and generating profound connections among those present, within themselves, and through the energy and breath of Spirit. The impact of the presence of the Spirit of the fullness of life was a newness of being that increased in its intensity on Pentecost and remains a vital presence for all who seek the intimacy and enlivening presence of Spirit.

Spirit remains our conduit or means of connection to the loving en-ergy of the divine. It is our lifeline, source of intuitive wisdom, and ever present companion to our Self. As the means of relationality between Self and the divine, Spirit can have an integral role in guiding living organisms towards a life of resiliency, courage, harmony, compassion, and attunement. The qualities that offer the hope of recovery from traumatic wounding and overwhelm and resiliency towards living more aligned with the potential of each individual's gifts and talents are the resources available to us through attuned and enhanced connection with Spirit. Complete and fulfilled lives are not a matter of meeting goals of material gain, renown, or productivity. Rather, fulfillment of life is in caring for the wounds that keep us bound in fear, growing in trust of Self, and allowing our unburdened internal family of parts to flourish as they authentically are. The more fully we align our internal system with Self and with Spirit by caring for the wounds and fears of parts, the greater our capacity is to respond with appropriate empathy and compassion to the suffering in the world, trust the wisdom of our intuitive knowing, and access resources for creative imagination and resiliency.

Fullness of life that is attuned to the Spirit of divine presence reflects qualities of Spirit in our relational life and self-understanding. The "fruits of the Spirit"—love, joy, peace, patience, kindness, generosity, faithfulness, gentleness, and self-control—identified in Paul's letter to the community at Galatia (Gal 5:22–23 NRSV) are one cataloging of the qualities of life lived in attunement with divine Spirit. They parallel the qualities of Self from the IFS model (compassion, creativity, calmness, clarity, connectedness, confidence, curiosity, and courage). These qualities of life illuminated by both traditions of healing, health, and wisdom invite us to imagine a life of attuned empathy, connected relationality, compassionate care of self and others, and self reservation emerging from a trust that there can be enough.

Trust in the sufficiency of enough can be challenging in a cultural environment that runs on perceptions of scarcity and the need of those with access to acquire and horde resources thereby generating social crisis of resource inequality and abuses of economic power. The anxiety of scarcity and the real experiences of scarcity for increasing percentages of our local and global communities indicate the presence of overfunctioning, fear based strategies that betray and impede the presence of the Spirit. When we choose to energize parts who perpetuate strategies of harm out of their own fear rather than care for their wounds with compassion, we participate in diminishing the flow and vitality of Spirit presence in our lives and the world. Like the divine power of the first person of the Trinity, Spirit does not exert unilateral power or influence. Instead, Spirit offers the unceasing promise of holistic, fulfilling, compassionate companionship and attuned loving connection to divine energy that is present in all.

GATHERING TOGETHER AS COMMUNITY: AN ECCLESIOLOGY

When Spirit is present and flowing through the relational connections within and among us, healthy community begins to emerge. For the followers of Jesus who were present on Pentecost, community began to flourish as language barriers were dissolved and was reimagined as care for all persons in community. Care for community took on greater importance than simply care of the individual or immediate family. The expanded recognition of the intricate and rich web of connections made possible by the illumination of the Spirit of life beckons us towards living in a way that honors the life of the Spirit in others. This reality of the ontological connections of divine energy among living beings, in the world, and with God guides our theological confessions regarding community identification, formation, and inclusion. At its most basic form, community is simply the gathering together of two or three (Matt 18:20) or the joining with others with the intention of sharing the presence of divine energy and grace. The sharing of divine presence and energy with others is visible in the optimal relationality and care of the imminent Trinity, the connected attunement between Spirit and Self, the curious compassion of building trust and restoration among Self and internal parts, the honoring of alterity and extension of respect in the interpersonal relationships of family and society, and the balance of sustenance and flourishing in our planet's environment. When we enter into the sharing of divine presence and relationship, we join into the community of God.

Inclusion in the full community of God does not require membership at a religious house of worship or belief in a prescribed set of theological doctrines. It is not about denominational organizations or joining the "right" church. The full community of God is available to all through the acknowledgement and honoring of divine energy and presence in life. Where we find the sacred presence of life, even in its most rudimentary forms, we find a companion in the community of God. Companionship in community is a beautiful gift when we are able to look past our own experiences of sin that distort or disrupt our capacity to acknowledge divine presence within our self and in others. Communing with divine presence is as close to our being as the breath of Spirit that flows through our body. It is as integral to our being and life in the world as our cells are to our body. When we begin to limit our awareness of divine energy and presence out of our own fear or misconceptions, we begin to segment our self, our relationships, our society, and our world into those who are enough like us and can be welcomed and included and those whose difference exceeds our capacity for empathy and hospitality. The struggle to care for and ease our fears and woundings that cause us to exclude and deny the presence of God within an other is the work of growing in enriching attunement with divine energy and presence through the Spirit of the fullness of life. Community, whether of our internal multiplicity, external relationality, or global environment, provides each of us with unceasing opportunities to engage in the work of growing empathetic, attuned attachments that allow us to see the presence of the divine with greater clarity and care.

The primary task of community is make us increasingly aware of the connections that bind and hold us with care and a desire for harmony and fulfillment. None of us exist as a singular, fully autonomous individual. We all depend on the work and care of others from infancy to death to grow, develop, cultivate meaning, meet basic needs, and fulfill our innate desires and talents for life. The image of the fully "self-made man" is a fallacy and can only be promoted through the active disregard of the care and work of others. We are a product of our connections, for good and for harm, just as we utilize our power within connections and attachments to influence the quality of our relational worlds. If we can acknowledge the presence and quality of our relational attachments and take care in how we utilize our relational power, we have the potential to craft attachments that lead towards authenticity and reduce the relational injuries that cause harm and strategies of increasingly rigid protection.

As we each become more present to the vulnerable parts within our internal system, we have the opportunity to offer restorative care to our internal parts and then extend that same care to the vulnerable ones in our midst. Caring for vulnerable ones in our society, those who suffer from the wounds of abuses of power of any form, including systemic oppression and trauma, is what Jesus directs us towards throughout his public ministry as he instructs us to care for the "least of these." From the Sermon on the Mount and Beatitudes to the formation of the community in Acts, Jesus consistently and regularly joined with the work of the Spirit in caring for those who were ill, vulnerable, poor, cast out, grieving, or injured by those who abuse the power granted to them. He restores sight to the blind, generates communities of hope and healing, reminds us of the blessings of mercy, peace, compassion, and justice, and encourages those who follow him, love him, or seek to silence him to choose right relationality over personal expediency. The community formed on Pentecost by the full infusion of the Spirit responded to the presence of divine attachment by extending Jesus' model of care as a model of community marked by sufficiency and generosity. "All who believed were together and had all things in common; they would sell their possessions and goods and distribute the proceeds to all, as any had need. Day by day, as they spent much time together in the temple, they broke bread at home and ate their food with glad and generous hearts, praising God and having the goodwill of all the people"(Acts

2:44–47 NRSV). Communities devoted to enhancing attachments to divine Spirit and caring connections with the vulnerable ones in our midst more fully reflect the qualities of vibrancy, health, and authenticity found through the presence of divine presence and energy.

Healthy and compassionate communities that foster resiliency and healing attachments share many of the same qualities found in the fruits of the Spirit or Self leadership. The presence of these characteristics is an outflow of connection to divine presence and is manifest across the world's cultures and religious traditions. Compassion, peace, joy, courage, clarity, patience, wisdom, and creativity are not just Christian qualities; moreso, they are not restricted to a single denomination or congregation. The presence of divine energy and flow of Spirit transcends the many cultural manifestations of religious and spiritual traditions. However, this does not mean that the particularities of our traditions and local communities are unimportant. The qualities of Spirit are universal but the connections we cultivate as opportunities to experience attachment and practice healthful uses of relational power are incredibly specific and concrete. Our communities of attachment are formative of who we are and can either facilitate or hinder our growth towards resiliency and health. Religious and spiritual communities that utilize their wisdom traditions, rituals, and relational attachments to welcome all persons and parts of persons generate environments that foster healing and authentic full lives. Those that use their sacred texts, theological traditions, and rituals in theologically abusive ways that promote feelings of shame, guilt, or fear add to the wounding of persons and the dishonor of the church and faith tradition. Like the moneychangers in the Temple who initiate the righteous anger of Jesus or the practice of the sale of indulgences that lit the fire of Reformation, there will continue to be individuals and groups who are more interested in perverting traditions of healing, intentionally or without conscious awareness, to feed their own burdens of wealth or power acquisition. How communities cultivate discernment and establish boundaries around abuses of relational power are essential to forming communing relationships with the potential and hope of enhancing our attachments to Self, one another, and divine presence.

TRAUMA SENSITIVE ETHICS

The relational connections that we form and live through in communities provide opportunities for greater personal awareness, challenges to our assumptions about the world, and resources for mending prior wounds. The boundaries, norms, and guidelines that shape our communal expectations and experiences can have a significant impact on whether the attachments we cultivate in community contribute to further abuses of power and wounding or if they contribute to resiliency and empathetic attunement with Self, others, and divine presence. The guidelines of how we comport ourselves in relation to others is the realm of ethics. For people of faith, the quality of our relationality and presence in the world optimally draws inspiration from our theological confessions.

Our most deeply held beliefs and values always inform our choices of how to act and relate in the world. The thing or value we most cherish will become the center of our life and relationships and determine how we make the choices that impact our life and relationships. Tillich discusses faith as "the state of being ultimately concerned" and as "an act of the total personality. It happens in the center of the personal life and includes all its elements. Faith is the most centered act of the human mind."[6] Faith, for Tillich, is not an exclusively religious phenomena but designates the fervor and primacy of whatever is the central focus of a person's life. This center could be following Jesus; more often, it is "family," "success," "winning," "fame," "patriotism/nationalism," "money/financial independence," "fun," "happiness," or any of the multitude of other commitments that function to center a person's life and order their decisions. The choice of how and on what we center our lives is our personal "religion"; it is the center around which we order our lives, relationships, and decisions. Whether or not we choose our center with intentional awareness, our lives will reflect the content of our center and faith.

For individuals who regularly participate in communities of faith, the theology articulated in sermons, liturgy, rituals, songs, and rhythms of social interaction will influence one's center and subsequent decisions and ethics. If God is distant, transcendent, unmoved, omnipotent, and requires obedience, then our ethics will reflect a use of power that is static, demanding, and not impacted by suffering. If God is active, present, intimate, emerging, and desires relationship, then our ethics will reflect those qualities of divine presence. If God is engaged in waging a war against the adversary at all costs, then our ethical positions will reveal an underlying perspective of us versus them and good versus evil without space for complication, context, or ambiguity. When we sing of the cosmic war, earthly war is an inevitable

---

6. Paul Tillich, *Dynamics of Faith*, 1, 4.

and understandable reality. When we raise our voices in the psalms of lament, we increase our capacity for compassion and empathy. When we join the choruses in streets or pews in songs of hope and freedom, we cultivate our awareness of the presence of oppression in our society and the need to be in solidarity with those who experience systematic forms of abuses of power that diminish wellbeing. The concrete expression of our faith in preaching, liturgy, hymnody, and rituals all have the capacity to craft the quality of the central and ultimate concern of our life and our priorities.

The ultimate concern that functions as the centering priority of our life is expressed through our decision making processes and choices. H. Richard Niebuhr offers three forms of ethical deliberation: person-the-maker, person-the-citizen, and person-the answerer.[7] The first form centers on the concern for teleology, or the goal. Ethical mandates and norms of social behavior are established according to how well they contribute to the fulfillment of a vision or goal. The second form is deontological, or with regard of the law. Within this form, adherence to the law is the highest good and the ideal criteria for behavior. The third form centers on responsiveness. Moral behavior, according to this type, is neither static nor predetermined. Rather, a moral and appropriate response takes into account the dynamic dimensions of the context and reply with the most fitting and compassionate answer. While noting the contexts in which the first two forms are beneficial, Niebuhr clearly advocates for the third form as the moral grounds for ethical behavior. Responsible moral action includes four elements: response or call to moral action, interpretation of the call, accountability for the outcome of action, and presence of social solidarity.[8] Moving through each phase in considering the appropriate response for moral action generates space for concerns such as compassion, wellbeing, and resiliency.

Cultivating a Niebuhrian response-ability approach to moral ethics is a helpful model for trauma-sensitive ethics. Trauma-sensitive theology and Niebuhr's responsible self share commitments towards recognition of alterity, multiplicity, contextuality, accountability, empathy, and conscious awareness of interpretative lenses. Moral and ethical response is far more complicated than static systems of rule following and goal achievement permit. When we are guided by teleology or the desire to meet a predetermined

---

7. Niebuhr, *The Responsible Self*. Language altered from "man" to "person" in order to be more inclusive.

8. Ibid., 61–65.

goal, we are more likely to disregard those who may impede progress towards the desired end or utilize our power in abusive ways to meet the goal. In our complicated world that increasingly pits wealth acquisition against needs for survival, the ends frequently do not justify the means. Likewise, legal behavior is not always moral behavior. The legally justified shooting of unarmed persons continues to plague American society and rightfully generate moral outrage at the blatant disregard for appropriate uses of power. When we fix our moral compasses on the relatively static measures of teleology and deontology, we open ourselves up to greater risks of perpetrating abuses of power and traumatizing wounding by prioritizing the goal or law over the particularities of the context. This does not mean that ethics and morality are wholly relativistic. There are guidelines, commitments, priorities, and boundaries that direct a response morality.

Akroatic Embodied Hearing as Spiritual Practice

In order to delineate an ethics of responsiveness, we first must cultivate practices of attuned presence and hearing. Attunement requires fully embodied presence with awareness of the multitude of means of communication, including verbal and the non-verbal communication forms of movement, posture, affect, energy resonance, and timing. Attending to the various dimensions of interpersonal interaction beckons us towards our somatic wisdom and intuition. Somatic wisdom and intuition draws on our entire sensory and resonate capacities to move us towards akroatic embodied hearing. What is akroatic embodied hearing? "Akroatic" is a term employed by Lisbeth Lipari[9] and derives from interdisciplinary study of sound and the action of listening. Most simply, akroatic hearing is attunement to harmony and rhythm. Listening is not simply a matter of attention or of the mechanism of sound reception and interpretation; rather listening is a fully somatic engagement in which one attends to the multidimensionality of communication. Akroatic embodied hearing and presence is receptive to the flow of emotional energy, aware of one's own internal somatic life, and inviting of the many non-verbal means of being present with self, others, and/or the divine.[10] Like any other spiritual discipline or practice of care, akroatic embodied hearing of the presence and flow of divine energy requires intentional awareness and development of skills of attunement to

9. Lipari, *Listening, Thinking, Being.*

10. Baldwin, *Sensing Sacred,* 72–88.

the variable presence and quality of the affective energy of parts and Self within and then the gradual expansion through empathy of attuning to the emotional energy of others.

When we attune, or literally tune-in, to our emotional and spiritual lives and resources, a larger world of connection begins to unfold as we become more aware of divine presence in our life and in the lives of all living beings. The opening up of the world of connections brings additional awareness of how our internal systems can resonate with the emotional lives of others, as if their emotional presence has the capacity to reach into our system and activate similar emotional responses as we energetically vibrate together. As you recall from our conversation about ontology and divine power at the beginning of the systematic, constructive theology section, all that is is energy, either bound into material or mass or free energy connecting and moving through everything. Whenever we begin working with the language of energetic connection, we eventually need to explore the qualities of those connections. How do we notice the grounded peace of Self presence within? In what ways does that feel different in sensation, affect, or posture than the blending presence of parts that hold wounds or seek to take the lead in pro-social strategies for life? What visceral sensation connects with the emotions of sorrow, anxiety, fear, contentment? As we become more fluent in our own attention to sensations, affect, parts, Self, and divine presence, how do we then more fully utilize our capacity for empathy? How can I feel with my client or parishioner or partner in order to be more fully present to their needs while also maintaining my energetic boundary that keeps us from becoming merged with the overwhelming affect of others?

Cultivating an awareness of our Self requires a return to the somatic awareness of our body. Just as the second person required incarnation as the embodied Jesus to more fully grow in empathy and connection with life in the created order, we too require a return to the deep wellspring of wisdom that resides through our bodies. All of our knowing, as perception, sensation, or intuition, is received through the somatic wisdom of our embodiment. Unfortunately, most of our cultural mandates take us away from the grounded, innate wisdom of our body center. From our increasing dependence on technology and media to pursuits of sculpting our bodies for appearance or function without pausing to connect and hear the needs and desires of our body. Perhaps counterintuitively, enriching our connection to divine presence requires cultivating practices of embodied hearing and witness. What do I mean by embodied hearing and witness? Embodied hearing is a spiritual practice of fully embodied, open and active means of attunement to Self, internal parts, others, and the divine that opens up new ways of being and thinking about religious, secular, and personal interaction. It is a transrational approach to knowing in which our cognitive processes take on the role of partner in knowing rather than leader. When our cognitive, linguistic, linear skills that become so well developed in our contemporary society and educational systems learn to function in partnership with the kinesthetic, affective, proprioceptive, interoceptive, and intuitive dimensions of knowing awareness we are able to experience a more holistic and complete epistemology.

The expansion of our ways of knowing is always available to us if we have the desire to explore beyond what our cultural norms of substance, materialism, and disembodied rationality assert as normative and solely important. A return to the wisdoms of the body, sensation, intuition, felt sense of connections, tracking the multidimensionality of parts expression in our internal system, the compassionate care between Self and parts, and the flow of energy emanating from those around us has the potential to deepen and expand our awareness and care of self and enhance harmony in our communities and world.

Conclusion

Inviting Cohesion

The primary aim of Trauma-Sensitive Theology is to offer a way of thinking through the many loci of our theological systems that honors the experience of traumatic wounding, takes care to reduce the potential for further wounding through abuses of theological, religious, or spiritual power, and offers theological language for the fostering of resiliency. As such, this is a theology for the ecclesia of survivors and those who offer care. It is not centered on reinforcing centers and structures of religious or denominational power or "explaining the faith" for the purpose of gaining converts and influence. Trauma-sensitive theology has a preferential option for those who suffer and experience traumatic wounding. It seeks to offer a theological balm for the wounds of trauma and illuminate a path towards resiliency, healing, and restoration of connection and balance.

Our path began with an affirmation of the importance of theological thinking and practice. For many survivors of trauma of any form—primary, secondary, intergenerational, societal, and cultural, connection to their faith tradition is important and can be a resource for stability and recovery. However, for others, the experience of trauma and subsequent disconnections pose significant challenges when our theologies are ill-equipped to offer an adequate accounting of God's role in the world and events of traumatic overwhelm and wounding. Constructing a theological response to trauma is essential as incidences of trauma are increasingly visible and broadcast internationally. We began this task by imagining ontology through the lens of energy rather than substance. If God is the source of life giving, loving energy that is manifest in the bounded energy of matter and the free energy of relational connections, then God's influence in the world is both intimate and contingent. The contingency of divine influence is based on whether or not each entity or organism attunes to divine energy or blocks connection in Self-protection through parts who cut us off in an effort to protect Self. This reflects divine uses of power that are invitational and relational rather than directive and unilateral. God's demonstration of invitational power that honors the integrity and dignity of others within the Trinity and in creation is a model for human uses of power that value consent, mutuality, and care for others. For survivors of trauma, consensual uses of power with a care for mutuality and the dignity of each party is essential for offering an alternative to the type of power that generated traumatic wounding.

Narratives of creation offered in trauma-sensitive theology shift the focus from traditional conceptualizations of the power of divine fiat in making perfection from nothing to a doctrine of creation that acknowledges that we all emerge from something and that the somethings of our beginnings are messy, elemental, chaotic, and deep. For survivors, the task of re/forming oneself after traumatic wounding often resonates more with the messy generation of order and balance from the chaos than it does the pronouncement of perfection. Human beings, while created with intimacy of connection via divine breath of Spirit and in reflection of the divine multiplicity or plurality of Elohim, genuinely struggle with the wildness of existence. We all live in this space bumping into each other, offering care, and seeking to find our proverbial feet. The task of growing in authentic practices of resonance and attunement within ourself and with others is challenging—and we often mess up and some of our mess ups are traumatizing. We use our relational power in efforts to cultivate meaning for our lives, meet our needs, and protect our Self from wounding. However, in our efforts to protect, we frequently wound. The grace modeled in the life of the embodied Jesus and the offering of divine Spirit is the hope of care and restoration. Each of us has the potential to use our relational power in ways that facilitate wellbeing . . . but we also have to engage in the work of caring for our internal wounds. Restoration of divinely offered life giving connection begins with our own internal journeys of offering care to the injured and to the protective parts within.

Salvation, or healing, does not emerge like magic through the joining of the right community, performance of the right spiritual tasks, or an acceptance of further wounding in attempts to model the suffering or death of Jesus. Healing does not come through further infliction of trauma. Rather, it is the outflow of establishing reconnection with Self and Spirit, offering healing unburdening of our own internal parts, allowing parts to assume their authentic gifts of flourishing, and enhancing our attuned connections with God and Self, and extending that grace to others. Cultivating resilien-cy and recovery from traumatic wounding requires care of all dimensions of who we are. In order to participate in the binding and soothing of the wounds of traumatic violation and injury, theology must resist its history of valorizing suffering and death and renew its commitment as a resource of healing and inspiration of healthy behavior and relational attachments. The renewal of commitment towards theological construction that answers to the needs and reflects a compassionate witnessing and embodied hearing reception of the wounds of the community is part of the response-ability of the theologian and spiritual care provider.

Theologians, clergy, and spiritual care providers have an active respon-sibility and role within the community of faith and in the world. As arbiters and proclaimers of our religious traditions, rituals, and sacred texts, it is not enough to rest on the declarations of faith from hundreds or thousands of years ago. While the core narrative of our faith may not change in regards to its objective content, how we tell the story and enact it though our liturgy and practices of care must shift in resonance with our times. Metaphors, symbols, and models that once communicated the intention of writers in the era of Abraham, Hagar, and Joseph differ from those of John of Patmos, Paul, or Mary. Likewise, the ways in which we communicate the central themes of faith require an updating for each cultural epoch. The primary lens of concern for theology of each cultural era reflects the dynamics and needs of the time. Trauma-sensitive theology argues that the most pressing concern for our era is the prevalence of trauma exposure and response at both clinical and subclinical intensities. Left to fester on its own and with-out care, the wounds of trauma present in individuals, communities, and our society will amplify and become increasingly extreme, rigid, and polar-ized. The current fervor of xenophobia, rise of extremism at either ends of our political spectrum (specifically the emboldening of the alt-right in America), latent PTSD fueling lethal over-responses by first responders, increasing tribalism and us-versus-them binaries, and increased presence of generalized anxiety and concern for future wellbeing is a reflection of traumatic response at the level of society and culture.

Trauma sensitive community leaders and care providers have a re-sponsibility to examine our professional practices as to how they either facilitate the entrenchment of protective strategies or the cultivation of Self-led social engagement and care. Let us recall David Blumenthal's ar-ticulation of the role of the theologian. "To be a theologian is to be on the boundary." Theologians of the boundary embody care for multiple responsibilities including "to be a voice for the tradition, speak for God, defend God, speak for one's fellow human beings, be in solidarity with one's fellow human beings before God, speak the 'ought', and have prior commitments." Our commitments as leaders of faith communities, theologians, and care providers require us to remain able to respond with care and compassion to a great variety of human needs while also balancing our mandate to reflect our spiritual and religious traditions authentically. Sometimes speaking well on behalf and in defense of God means updating the content of our traditions. Sometimes being a voice for our traditions requires us to insist on the renewal of forgotten or diminished ritual practices of health. Sometimes speaking the "ought" requires us to stand up against structures of power that do not honor divine presence in the world and inflict traumatizing wounds on entire portions of our national or global community. Sometimes being in solidarity with one's fellow human being means meeting a survivor of assault in the emergency room and holding her hand through procedures that can feel like revictimization. Taking on the vocation and role of theologian, clergy, or care provider requires attending to a host of commitments while always keeping the primacy of health and resiliency in focus.

INCORPORATING CARE

Self care

Providing care for the wounds within our own being or in our communities requires a balance of knowledge, empathy, and presence. My clinical mentor at times reminds me that what is most required is simply "to be a highly-educated, regular self." Her intention is to bring to the foreground that knowledgeable presence coupled with an openness for healthy attachment is frequently the most grace-filled gift we can offer another person or being. It is the embodiment of the offering of connection to divine energy and presence. When I can care for my parts and resonate with Self energy within my embodied being, I have the potential to offer that care as a touchstone for others to resonate alongside.

Self care is a popular buzz word in our current culture—with good reasons. The colloquial use generally points us towards practices of rejuvenation and relaxation. Blogs, magazines, and self help books all encourage us to engage in self care that generally includes nurturing our bodies through regular movement, healthy eating, or indulging in a dietary or spa related luxury. Self care that encourages us towards care of body, spirit, mind, and attachments is a good thing, especially for clergy who tend to neglect care of self. Additionally, self care is a bit different than Self care, or care of parts by Self. Self care is the open, loving, healing witnessing of the wounds of our hurt and protective parts and offer of redemptive and resurrection compassion. It includes identifying our internal parts, offering curiosity and appreciation of how and why they perform the roles they do in our life, and extending connection to divine presence and energy that flows from God through Spirit to Self for unburdening and restoration of the innate gifts of parts. While Self care may include some of the strategies of self care, the intention and scope of care differs significantly. Care through Self energy and Self leadership is the hope of salvation and the restoration of our authentic being. Healthy care of and attachments with others begins with care and healthy attachments between parts and Self within us. The degree to which we can offer our parts Self care will set the bar for our capacity to offer care to others.

Boundaries as Care

Healthy attachments that facilitate care and connection require healthy boundaries. Boundaries often either get misinterpreted as walls or activate pushback from caretaking or people pleasing parts who believe that affirmation from others requires us to be boundary-less or exiles that fear disconnection. Boundaries are the structure that allows healthy and functional attachments to occur. Like I describe to my clients, boundaries are like "holding the frame" in ballroom dance. As you may recall from the movie, *Dirty Dancing*, as Johnny teaches Baby how to dance (instead of just stepping on his feet), he sets the frame of their arms and says something to the effect of "This is your dance space (gesturing to her side of the frame) and this is my dance space (gesturing to his side)." As they set and hold the frame of the dance, they are able to more fully and impressively dance together without injury. Boundaries are what allow our connections within our self and with others to dance. And, like dance partnerships, sometimes the form of the boundaries change in order to accommodate a different kind of relationship or a different genre or form of dance partnership. They are not walls of disconnection or structure-less mounds of relational enmeshments. Rather, they are the variety of relational structures that facilitate a great variety of relational attachments and connections.

Understanding the role and various types of boundaries are essential for care of trauma. Many times, traumatic wounding occurs because of a violation of appropriate boundaries either out of intention or ignorance. Understanding and communicating our role with clarity is an essential component of establishing boundaries that are the foundation of generating enough safety for the care of trauma. While the basic safety and privacy dimensions of appropriate professional boundaries are generally well known and shared across care giving professions, it is helpful to be clear with self and care receivers about the scope of care, availability of care in the midst of subjective or objective crisis, and limits of care. Additionally, it is important to hold the boundaries, with the clarity that holding of boundaries is for safety and stability and never punishment. Boundaries within the realm of congregational leadership differ from those of pastoral care and counseling, and both differ from the clinical relationship. The difference in boundaries is largely due to the degree of personal information and emotional intimacy present in the various relationships. The more intimacy and vulnerability that is present for care on the part of the care receiver the more protected the boundaries need to be to generate enough safety to engage in the work of the relationship.

While we most often think of boundaries in the context of the care professions, boundaries are present in all types of relationships—they are what gets crossed in abuses of relational power or sin. Boundaries set the guidelines for the accepted and mutually agreed upon norms of the relationship. Sometimes we are personally involved in establishing these norms, other times, they are established by our society. Social norms dictate that I pay for goods and services and treat others in the public with a certain level of respect. Personal norms determine how I am willing to be treated by friends, family, or colleagues. The norms inform our consent of touch, language choices, expectation of disclosures of personal information, etc. Relational norms and boundaries are present in our social interactions, professional services, interpersonal connections, and internal care of parts.

Do No Harm

The choice to offer care to our parts, others in our midst, or our larger community is a tremendous gift and responsibility. It is a gift to be allowed into relationship during our most vulnerable times and experiences. It is a sacred trust that warrants proper attention and care. When we awaken to the depth of vulnerability of exiled parts, whether within our personal internal system or within the system of others, it becomes clear that care-taking requires an awareness of the dynamics and path of recovery from wounding. Becoming educated as to the features of human vulnerability, wounding, and trauma is motivated by the mandate and desire to "do no harm." Growing in our understanding of the prevalence, types, and impact of traumatic wounding helps us offer more attuned care. Compassionate awareness of the ways in which traumatic response allows us to interpret the signs of distress and respond appropriately and with a reduction in the risk of adding injuries. Trauma-sensitive theology and this text specifically are offered with the intention of shepherding care providers towards be-coming a more "highly-educated, regular self" with a keener eye towards care for traumatic wounding, response, processing, and resiliency.

When we begin to offer care to others in the context of pastoral care, congregational leadership, or theologically attentive psychotherapy, it is essential to establish with clarity the type of helping relationship we are equipped and trained to offer. Knowing the limits of our capacity to offer support for the care and recovery of traumatic wounding and the areas in which our capacities shine require awareness and discernment. There is room in the caring of wounded souls and communities for a great variety of talents and capabilities. Trauma-sensitive theology and praxis clearly blends two areas of professional formation, each with their own valuable offerings and skill sets. For clergy and pastoral care providers, learning about trauma response and recovery is likely a new area while exploring the ways in which a congregant's faith informs their life and capacity for resiliency is more familiar. For therapists, the learning edge may be in how to assess the way in which religious practice and personal theology func-tions for the client while assessing trauma response is already a part of your practice. In both cases, the most basic commitment is to do no harm.

The two most common areas in which harm occurs on the religious and theological side are when we mistake the signs and symptoms of traumatic wounding as indicative of a lack of faith or moral fortitude and when our homiletics, teaching, and liturgy unreflectively promote uses of power and social practices that contribute to sin and abuses of relational power. Trauma-sensitive theology seeks to mitigate the risk of theological or spiritual abuse of power by offering an alternative vision of divine power and presence, theological anthropology, and the dynamics between sin and salvation. These theological offerings are a response to our growing awareness of the prevalence of traumatic wounding at all levels of our society and a sensitivity towards the impact of trauma on our biological, somatic, psychological, relational, and spiritual being. As congregational leaders and spiritual care givers, we have a responsibility, or response-ability, to offer informed care in our direct contacts with congregants and through our public statements. When we offer a compassionate and courageous welcoming of alterity and multiplicity from our positions of oratory power, we encourage empathy and accountability in our communities. Likewise, when we perpetuate theological models that valorize suffering and abuse or reinforce social structures of unilateral power as domination, we fuel sin.

Therapists are at risk of unintentionally causing harm when we underestimate or dismiss the importance and function of our client's personal theologies. Our role is not to judge the content of our client's faith; rather, it is to assess how that content functions in the life of our client. Does the content of faith contribute to further traumatic wounding and overwhelm or is it a resource for resiliency? Assessing the role of faith in contributing to wounding or resiliency often means looking for underlying indications of the use of divine power, assumptions about the nature of humanity, models for salvation or new life, and quality and hope of fulfillment. Because the theology we believe is the society and life we will get, how our religious communities and how we as individuals engage these questions of power, human nature, sin, and salvation will show up in our relationships, hope for our future, and how we cope with challenges and injuries from our past. Our personal theologies, as distinct from the formal theological confessions and creeds of our traditions, are indicative of how we orient our lives, make decisions, and engage in relational attachments. Clinicians who can assess and engage clients in cultivating personal theologies that reflect their desires for healthy relationality and care of all parts, within and among, by Self and Spirit leadership, assist in the overall health and resiliency of those in our care. Faith matters—even when it is a rejection of traditional forms of religious practice and thought.

Attuned Care

Experiences of trauma, by definition, overwhelm an individual's capacity to cope and process the event in the moment. Like a skilled musician tuning an instrument to play a masterpiece, care of parts within our own internal multiplicity or segments of our community and society deserves knowledgeable, skilled, and attuned partners on the journey of recovery and resiliency. The nuts-and-bolts knowledge of the impact of traumatic wounding and the trajectory of traumatic response, processing, and recovery is an essential first step in offering companionship and care. We are fundamentally unable to offer support and guidance in areas in which we are a novice or uninformed. Second, we must take the time, attention, intention, and effort to hone our skills of recognizing symptoms of traumatic hyper-arousal and hypo-arousal, caring for our own parts that are activated by narratives of harm, and tracking the presence of various parts in those to whom we offer care. Third, we need to cultivate our own somatic awareness, wisdom, and resonance in order to then attune to the quality of energy of another. Tuning in to the presence of divine energy through Self and care of our own internal system allows us to more authentically, compassionately, and fully hold enough Self energy and, through somatic resonance, to offer enough safety and stability to others. The work of offering attuned, wise care starts with our own journey and Self care of parts.

Attuned care is care of the whole person—body, affect, energy, thoughts, relationality, and spirit. The primary commitments informing trauma-sensitive theology can serve as a lens and starting place for offering attuned and holistic care and fostering resiliency and recovery from traumatic wounding. They are the priority of bodily experience, full acceptance of trauma narratives, natural given-ness of human psychological multiplicity, and faith in the robust resiliency of trauma survivors. These four commitments provide a foundation for attuned, informed, compassionate care that can attend to all dimensions of traumatic wounding. First, honoring the dignity and experience of the body and placing in a space of priority acknowledges the ways in which our body was wounded, holds the impact of the wounds until we reach a place of enough safety, and provides many of the innate resources and mechanisms we need to process traumatic experiences. Our bodies are remarkable, wise, and deserving of grace and gratitude—even when we feel betrayed by or alien to our bodies due to the wounds of trauma. Second, receiving the narrative of trauma is an honor and gift of vulnerability. Telling the story of violation and harm is always terrifying, even if only in part. As witnesses to the narratives our primary responsibility is to receive the story with full belief in the subjective experience of the event. Narratives of traumatic wounding, as told either from an exterior person or from an exiled part of self, reflect the event of trauma as it was experienced by the survivor or part who survived. Attuned care seeks to resonate with the subjective experience of the violation with appropriate boundaries, Self care, and without reservation or suspicion.

Third, in order to offer attuned care to our own system or another person or community, we must care for our own internal multiplicity. Once we can care for our own internal system with compassion, grace, and fluidity, we can model the health of Self leadership and internal harmony. All of us have parts. This is not a statement that reflects serious psychopathology or ontological brokenness; it is simply how we were created in the image of a triune, plural, relational presence. Each of us is more than a singular part of us. This recognition is often one of the first steps in cultivating resiliency. Claiming our natural, adaptive psychological multiplicity with confidence and clarity establishes a path towards harmony rather than singularity. Fourth, attuned care always holds the secure faith in the potential for recovery and resiliency. Just as the death of Jesus did not have the final word, traumatic wounding does not have the final word. The depth of the wounding and pain do matter; yet, the wounds of trauma are not the entirety of the survivor. Protected from the overwhelm of trauma remains resources for recovery, resiliency, compassion, grace, courage, love, creativity, playfulness, clarity, curiosity, and renewal. Feeling these qualities while in the midst of traumatic response and processing may, at times, feel impossible; however, they do remain. Part of the responsibility of offering attuned care is holding fiercely to the hope and promise of resiliency. The resources of resiliency can include our spiritual practices, rituals, community of faith, and even our theology.

A SURVIVOR'S CREED

I believe survivors of trauma,
In the promise of strength and resiliency.

I believe in God, divine energy and presence,
who draws into order the waters of the deep,
Spirit hovering in communion,
present at the gift of creation,
vivifying breath to the good and beloved human.

CONCLUSION

I believe in Jesus, the Christ,
fully Self led and vision of optimal relationality,
who experienced the full weight of trauma,
disconnected from the source of life,
resurrected, renewed, and offering the Spirit of life.

I believe in the welcoming of all parts,
the honor of the body,
the grace of companionship,
the healing of wounds,
the resurrection of the exiles,
and the renewal of authentic life. Amen.

Bibliography

Adams, Carole, ed. *Ecofeminism and the Sacred*. New York: Continuum, 1993.

Alexander, Jeffrey. *Trauma: A Social Reader*. Cambridge, UK: Polity, 2012.

American Psychological Association. Child Sexual Abuse: What Parents Should Know. http://www.apa.org/pi/families/resources/child-sexual-abuse.aspx.

American Psychological Association. *Diagnostic and Statistical Manual of Mental Disorders*, 4th ed., text review. Washington, DC: American Psychological Association, 2000.

Anda, Robert et. al. "The Enduring Effects of Abuse and Related Adverse Experiences in Childhood: A Convergence of Evidence from Neurobiology and Epidemiology." *European Archive of Psychiatry and Clinical Neuroscience* 256 (2006) 174–86.

Arel, Stephanie and Shelly Rambo. *Post-Traumatic Public Theology*. New York: Palgrave Macmillan, 2016.

Artress, Lauren. *Walking a Sacred Path: Rediscovering the Labyrinth as a Spiritual Practice*. New York: Riverhead, 2006.

Ashley, Benedict. *Theologies of the Body: Humanist and Christian*. Braintree, MA: National Catholic Bioethics Center, 1985.

Ashbrook, James and Carol Rausch Albright. *The Humanizing Brain: Where Religion and Neuroscience Meet*. Cleveland: Pilgrim, 1997.

Baldwin, Jennifer. *Embracing the Ivory Tower and Stained Glass Windows: A Festschrift in Honor of Archbishop Antje Jackelén*. Issues in Science and Religion Series. New York: Springer, 2016.

———. "Akroatic, Embodied Hearing and Presence as Spiritual Practice." In *Sensing Sacred: Exploring the Human Senses in Practical Theology and Pastoral Care*, edited by Jennifer Baldwin, 72–88. Lanham, MD: Lexington, 2016.

———. *Sensing Sacred: Exploring the Human Senses in Practical Theology and Pastoral Care*. Lanham, MD: Lexington, 2016.

Barbour, Ian G. *Religion and Science: Historical and Contemporary Issues*. New York: HarperCollins, 1997.

———. *When Science Meets Religion*. New York: HarperCollins, 2000.

Barth, Karl. *Church Dogmatics*. Volume 3/3. Translated by Geoffrey Bromiley. Edinburgh: T. & T. Clark, 1960.

Benjamin, Jessica. *Bonds of Love: Psychoanalysis, Feminism, and the Problem of Domination*. New York: Pantheon, 1988.

Beste, Jennifer. *God and the Victim: Traumatic Intrusions on Grace and Freedom*. Oxford: Oxford University Press, 2007.

Black, M. C., et. al. "The National Intimate Partner and Sexual Violence Survey (NISVS): 2010 Summary Report." Atlanta: National Center for Injury Prevention and Control, Centers for Disease Control and Prevention, 2011. http://www.cdc.gov/violenceprevention/pdf/nisvs_report2010-a.pdf.

Blodgett, Barbara J. *Constructing the Erotic: Sexual Ethics and Adolescent Girls.* Cleveland: Pilgrim, 2002.

Blumenthal, David R. *Facing the Abusing God: A Theology of Protest.* Louisville: Westminster John Knox, 1993.

Bowman, Katy. *Movement Matters: Essays on Movement Science, Movement Ecology, and the Nature of Movement.* Sequim, WA: Propriometrics, 2016.

Bradshaw, G. A., *Elephants on the Edge: What Animals Teach Us about Humanity.* New Haven: Yale University Press, 2009.

Bradshaw, G. A., and Allan Schore. "How Elephants are Opening Doors: Developmental Neuroethology, Attachment and Social Context." *Ethology* 113 (2007) 426–36.

Bradshaw, G. A., et. al. "Building an Inner Sanctuary: Complex PTSD in Chimpanzees." *Journal of Trauma & Dissociation* 9 (2008) 9–34.

Breuer, Josef, and Sigmund Freud. *Studies in Hysteria.* Translated and edited by James Strachey. New York: Basic Books, 2000.

Briginshaw, Valerie A. *Dance, Space, and Subjectivity.* New York: Palgrave, 2001.

Brock, Rita Nakashima. *Journeys By Heart: A Christology of Erotic Power.* New York: Crossroad, 1988.

Brock, Rita Nakashima, and Gabriella Lettini. *Soul Repair: Recovering from Moral Injury After War.* Boston: Beacon, 2012.

Brock, Rita Nakashima, and Rebecca Ann Parker. *Proverbs of Ashes: Violence, Redemptive Suffering, and the Search for What Saves Us.* Boston: Beacon, 2001.

Brown, Joanne Carlson, and Carole R. Bohn, eds. *Christianity, Patriarchy, and Abuse: A Feminist Critique.* Cleveland: Pilgrim, 1989.

Brown, Lyn Mikel, and Carol Gilligan. *Meeting at the Crossroads: Women's Psychology and Girls' Development.* New York: Random, 1992.

Brown, Warren, and Nancey Murphy. *Bodies and Souls, or Spirited Bodies.* Cambridge: Cambridge University Press, 2006.

Brown, Warren, Nancey Murphy, and H. Newton Malony, ed. *Whatever Happened to the Soul?: Scientific and Theological Portraits of Human Nature.* Minneapolis: Fortress, 1998.

Browning, Don S. *Atonement and Psychotherapy.* Philadelphia: Westminster, 1966.

Brueggemann, Walter. *An Introduction to the Old Testament: The Canon and Christian Imagination.* Louisville: Westminster John Knox, 2003.

———. *Theology of the Old Testament: Testimony, Dispute, Advocacy.* Minneapolis: Fortress, 1997.

Buchwald, Emilie, Pamela Fletcher, and Martha Roth, eds. *Transforming a Rape Culture.* Revised ed. Minneapolis: Milkweed, 2005.

Butler, Judith. *Senses of the Subject.* New York: Fordham University Press, 2015.

Calvin, John. *Institutes of the Christian Religion* (1559). Edited by John McNeill and translated by Ford Lewis Battles. Vols. 20–21 of the Library of Christian Classics. Philadelphia: Westminster, 1960.

Capps, Donald. *The Child's Song: The Religious Abuse of Children.* Louisville: Westminster John Knox, 1995.

Caputo, John. *The Weakness of God: A Theology of the Event*. Bloomington: Indiana University Press, 2006.

Carr, Anne E. *Transforming Grace: Christian Tradition and Women's Experience*. New York: Continuum, 1988.

Chopp, Rebecca. *The Power to Speak: Feminism, Language, God*. Eugene, OR: Wipf and Stock, 2002.

———. *Saving Work: Feminist Practices in Theological Education*. Louisville: Westminster, 1995.

Christ, Carol, and Judith Plaskow, eds. *Weaving the Visions: New Patterns in Feminist Spirituality*. New York: HarperCollins, 1989.

Classen, Constance. *A Cultural History of Touch*. Urbana: University of Illinois Press, 2012.

Clayton, Philip. *Mind and Emergence: From Quantum to Consciousness*. Oxford: Oxford University Press, 2004.

Coakley, Sarah, ed. *Religion and the Body*. New York: Cambridge University Press, 1997.

Cobb, John, and David Ray Griffin. *Process Theology: An Introductory Exposition*. Louisville: Westminster John Knox, 1976.

Coleman, Monica. *The Dinah Project: A Handbook for Congregational Response to Sexual Violence*. Cleveland: Pilgrim, 2004.

———. *Making a Way Out of No Way: A Womanist Theology*. Minneapolis: Fortress, 2008.

Conterio, Karen, Wendy Lader, and Jennifer Kingson Bloom. *Bodily Harm: The Breakthrough Healing Program for Self-Injurers*. New York: Hyperion, 1999.

Cooper-White, Pamela. *Braided Selves: Collected Essays on Multiplicity, God, and Persons*. Eugene: Cascade, 2011.

———. *The Cry of Tamar: Violence against Women and the Church's Response*, 2nd ed. Minneapolis: Fortress, 2012.

———. *Many Voices: Pastoral Psychotherapy in Relational and Theological Perspective*. Minneapolis: Fortress, 2007.

Cozolino, Louis. *The Neuroscience of Human Relationships: Attachment and the Developing Social Brain*. New York: Norton, 2004.

———. *The Neuroscience of Psychotherapy: Building and Rebuilding the Human Brain*. New York: Norton, 2002.

Daly, Mary. *Beyond God the Father: Toward a Philosophy of Women's Liberation*. Boston: Beacon, 1973.

———. *The Church and the Second Sex*. New York: Harper and Row, 1975.

Davis, Stephen T., ed. *Encountering Evil: Live Options in Theodicy*. Atlanta: John Knox, 1981.

De Waal, Frans. *The Age of Empathy: Nature's Lessons for a Kinder Society*. New York: Three Rivers, 2009.

Dirty Dancing, directed by Emile Ardolino, Great American Films Limited Partnership, 1987.

Earley, Jay. *Self-Therapy: A Step-by-Step Guide to Creating Inner Wholeness Using IFS, A New Cutting-Edge Therapy*. Minneapolis: Mill City, 2009.

Ellis, Marc. *Toward a Jewish Theology of Liberation: The Challenge of the 21st Century*, 3rd ed. Waco, TX: Baylor University Press, 2004.

Emerson, David. *Trauma-Sensitive Yoga in Therapy: Bringing the Body into Treatment*. New York: Norton, 2015.

Engle, Mary Potter. "Evil, Sin, and Violation of the Vulnerable." In *Lift Every Voice: Constructing Christian Theologies from the Underside*, edited by Susan Brooks Thistlethwaite and Mary Potter Engle, 159–72. Maryknoll: Orbis, 1998.

Evers, Dirk, Antje Jackelen, and Taede Smedes. *How Do We Know?: Understanding in Science and Theology*. London: T. & T. Clark, 2010.

Fackenheim, Emil. *To Mend the World: Foundations of Post-Holocaust Jewish Thought*. Indianapolis: Indiana University Press, 1994.

Fortune, Marie. *Sexual Violence: The Sin Revisited*. Cleveland: Pilgrim, 2005.

———. *Sexual Violence: The Unmentionable Sin*. Cleveland: Pilgrim, 1983.

Fosha, Diana. *The Transforming Power of Affect: A Model for Accelerated Change*. New York: Basic, 2000.

Friedman, Jaclyn and Jessica Valenti. *Yes means yes!: Visions of Female Sexual Power & a World Without Rape*. Berkeley, CA: Seal, 2008.

Frankl, Viktor. *Man's Search for Meaning*. New York: Pocket, 1975.

Freyd, Jennifer, and Anne DePrince, eds. *Trauma and Cognitive Science: A Meeting of Minds, Science, and Human Experience*. New York: Haworth, 2001.

Gibbs, Raymond. *Embodiment and Cognitive Science*. Cambridge: Cambridge University Press, 2005.

Gilligan, Carol, Annie G. Rogers, and Deborah L. Tolman, eds. *Women, Girls & Psychotherapy: Reframing Resistance*. New York: Haworth, 1991.

Gish, Elizabeth, and Sarah Peck. *On the Alter: "The Vagina Monologues" as a Site for Ritualized Liberatory Narrative*. Washington, DC: American Academy of Religion Annual Meeting, 2006.

Gunkel, Hermann. *Genesis*. Translated by Mark Biddle. Macon: Mercer University Press, 1997.

Hall, Douglas John. *The Cross in Our Context: Jesus and the Suffering World*. Minneapolis: Fortress, 2003.

Hartley, Linda. *Wisdom of the Body Moving: An Introduction to Body-Mind Centering*. Berkley, CA: North Atlantic, 1995

Hartshorne, Charles. *Omnipotence and other Theological Mistakes*. Albany: State University of New York Press, 1984.

Hefner, Philip. *Technology and Human Becoming*. Minneapolis: Fortress, 2003.

Herbine-Blank, Toni, Donna Kerpelman, and Martha Sweezy. *Intimacy from the Inside Out: Courage and Compassion in Couple Therapy*. New York: Routledge, 2016.

Herman, Judith. *Trauma and Recovery*. New York: Basic, 1997.

Heyward, Carter. *Saving Jesus From Those Who Are Right*. Minneapolis: Fortress, 1999.

———. *Touching Our Strength: The Erotic as Power and the Love of God*. San Francisco: Harper & Row, 1989.

Horowitz, Seth. *The Universal Sense: How Hearing Shapes the Mind*. New York: Bloomsbury, 2015.

Howes, David, ed. *Empire of the Senses: The Sensual Cultural Reader*. New York: Berg, 2005.

Irwin, Alexander C. *Eros Toward the World: Paul Tillich and the Theology of the Erotic*. Minneapolis: Fortress, 1991.

Jackelén, Antje. *The Dialogue Between Religion and Science: Challenges and Future Directions*. Kitchener, ON: Pandora, 2004.

———. "From Drama to Disco: On the Significance of Relationality in Science and Religion." *Currents in Theology and Mission* 28 (2001) 229–37.

———. *Time & Eternity: The Question of Time in Church, Science, and Theology*. West Conshohocken, PA: Templeton Foundation, 2005.

Johnson, Elizabeth. *She Who Is: The Mystery of God in Feminist Theological Discourse*. New York: Crossroad, 1992.

Johnson, William Stacy. "Rethinking Theology: A Postmodern, Post-Holocaust, Post-Christendom Endeavor." *Interpretation* 55 (January 2001) 5–18.

Jones, Serene. "Bounded openness: Postmodernism, Feminism, and the Church Today." *Interpretation* 55 (January 2001) 49–59.

———. *Trauma and Grace: Theology in a Ruptured World*, Louisville: Westminster John Knox, 2009.

Joshi, Paramjit, and Dianne Kaschak. "Exposure to Violence and Trauma: Questionnaire for Adolescents." *International Review of Psychiatry* 10 (1998) 208–15.

Keller, Catherine. *Apocalypse Now and Then: A Feminist Guide to the End of the World*. Boston: Beacon, 1996.

———. *Face of the Deep: A Theology of Becoming*. London: Routledge, 2003.

———. *On the Mystery: Discerning God in Process*. Minneapolis: Fortress, 2008.

Keller, Catherine, Michael Nausner, and Mayra Rivera, eds. *Postcolonial Theologies: Divinity and Empire*. St. Louis: Chalice, 2004.

Keller, Catherine, and Laurel Schneider, eds. *Polydoxy: Theology of Multiplicity and Relation*. London: Routledge, 2011.

Kelley, Sheila. "Let's Get Naked." Tedx American Rivera, 2012. http://tedxtalks.ted.com/video/Lets-Get-Naked-Sheila-Kelley-at.

Kelly, Loch. *Shift Into Freedom: The Science and Practice of Open-Hearted Awareness*. Boulder, CO: Sounds True, 2015.

Keshgegian, Flora A. *Time for Hope: Practices for Living in Today's World*. New York: Continuum, 2006.

Kierkegaard, Søren. *The Concept of Anxiety*. Edited and Translated by Reidar Thomte. Princeton: Princeton University Press, 1980.

Kim, Simone Sunghae. "Psychological Contours of Multicultural Feminist Hermeneutics: Hand and Relationality." *Pastoral Psychology* 55 (2007) 723–30.

Klonsky, E. D., and J. Muehlenkamp. "Self-Injury: A Research Review for the Practitioner." *Journal of Clinical Psychology: In Session*, 63 (2007) 1045–56.

Kohut, Heinz. *Self Psychology and the Humanities: Reflections on a New Psychoanalytic Approach*. New York: Norton, 1985.

LaCugna, Catherine Mowry, ed. *Freeing Theology: The Essentials of Theology in Feminist Perspective*. San Francisco: HarperCollins, 1993.

Lamb, Sharon. *The Secret Life of Girls: What Good Girls Really Do—Sex Play, Aggression, and Their Guilt*. New York: Free, 2001.

Leslie, Kristen. *When Violence is No Stranger: Pastoral Counseling with Survivors of Acquaintance Rape*. Minneapolis: Fortress, 2003.

Levine, Peter. *Waking the Tiger: Healing Trauma: The Innate Capacity to Transform Overwhelming Experiences*. Berkeley: North Atlantic, 1997.

Linder, Cynthia. *Varieties of Gifts: Multiplicity and the Well-Lived Pastoral Life*. New York: Rowman & Littlefield, 2016.

Lipari, Lisbeth. *Listening, Thinking, Being: Toward an Ethics of Attunement*. University Park: Pennsylvania State University Press, 2014.

Lorde, Audre. *Sister Outsider: Essays and Speeches*. Berkeley: Crossing, 1984.

Luther, Martin. "Heidelberg Disputation." In *Luther's Works, Volume 31: Career of the Reformer I*, edited by Harold Grimm and Helmut Lehman. Minneapolis: Fortress, 1957.

Manlowe, Jennifer L. *Faith Born of Seduction: Sexual Trauma, Body Image, and Religion.* New York: New York University Press, 1995.

Martin, Randy. *Critical Moves: Dance Studies in Theory and Politics.* Durham: Duke University Press, 1998.

McFague, Sallie. *Metaphorical Theology: Models of God in Religious Language.* Minneapolis: Fortress, 1982.

Means, J. Jeffrey. *Trauma and Evil: Healing the Wounded Soul.* Minneapolis: Fortress, 2000.

Miller, Alice. *Banished Knowledge: Facing Childhood Injuries.* Translated by Leila Vennewitz. New York: Anchor, 1990.

Miller-Karas, Elaine. *Building Resilience to Trauma: The Trauma and Community Resiliency Models.* New York: Routledge, 2015.

Miller-McLemore, Bonnie. *Let the Children Come,* San Francisco: Jossey-Bass, 2003.

Moltmann, Jürgen. *The Trinity and the Kingdom.* Minneapolis: Fortress, 1993.

Moore, Carol-Lynne, and Kaoru Yamamoto. *Beyond Words: Movement Observation and Analysis.* Second Edition. New York: Routledge, 2012.

Mount Shoop, Marcia. *Let the Bones Dance: Embodiment and the Body of Christ.* Louisville: Westminster John Knox, 2010.

Nelson, James B. *Body Theology.* Lousiville: Westminster John Knox, 1992.

Newberg, Andrew, and Eugene D'Aquili. *Why God Won't Go Away: Brain Science and the Biology of Belief.* New York: Ballantine, 2001.

Newell, Jason and Gordon MacNeil. "Professional Burnout, Vicarious Trauma, Secondary Traumatic Stress, and Compassion Fatigue: A Review of Theoretical Terms, Risk Factors, and Preventive Methods of Clinicians and Researchers." *Best Practice in Mental Health* 6 (Summer 2010) 57–68.

Niebuhr, H. Richard. *The Responsible Self: An Essay in Christian Moral Philosophy.* New York: Harper & Row, 1963.

Noddings, Nel. *Women and Evil.* Berkeley, CA: University of California Press, 1989.

NurrieStearns, Mary and Rick NurrieStearns. *Yoga for Emotional Trauma: Meditations and Practices for Healing Pain and Suffering.* Oakland, CA: New Harbinger, 2013.

Ogden, Pat, Kekumi Minton, and Clare Pain. *Trauma and the Body: A Sensorimotor Approach to Psychotherapy.* New York: Norton, 2006.

Pannenberg, Wolfhart. *Anthropology in Theological Perspective.* Translated by Matthew O'Connell. Edinburgh: T. & T. Clark, 1985.

Peres, Julio, et. al. "Spirituality and Resilience in Trauma Victims." *Journal of Religion and Health* 46 (2007) 343–50.

Peters, Ted. *God as Trinity: Relationality and Temporality in Divine Life.* Louisville: Westminster John Knox, 2003.

———. *Sin: Radical Evil in Soul and Society.* Reprint. Eugene, OR: Wipf and Stock, 2006.

Plaskow, Judith. *Sex, Sin and Grace: Women's Experience and the Theologies of Reinhold Niebuhr and Paul Tillich.* New York: University Press of America, 1980.

Poling, James. "Child Sexual Abuse: A Rich Context for Thinking about God, Community, and Ministry." *Journal of Pastoral Care* 42 (Spring 1988) 58–61.

———. *Deliver Us from Evil: Resisting Racial and Gender Oppression.* Minneapolis: Fortress, 1996.

———. *The Abuse of Power: A Theological Problem.* Nashville: Abingdon, 1991.

Pollard, Jennifer. "Seen, Seared, and Sealed: Trauma and the Visual Presentation of September 11." *Health, Risk and Society* 13 (February 2011) 81–101.

Porges, Stephen. *The Polyvagal Theory: Neurophysiological Foundations of Emotions, Attachment, Communication, and Self-Regulation.* New York: Norton, 2011.

Propper, Ruth, R. Stickgold, and S. Christmanl. "Is Television Traumatic?: Dreams, Stress and Media Exposure in the Aftermath of September 11, 2001." *Psychological Science* 18 (2007) 334–40.

Rambo, Shelly. *Spirit and Trauma: A Theology of Remaining.* Louisville: Westminster John Knox, 2010.

Redmond, Sheila. "Christian 'Virtues' and Recovery from Child Sexual Abuse." In *Christianity, Patriarchy, and Abuse,* edited by Joanne Carlson Brown and Carole Bohn. Cleveland: Pilgrim, 1989.

Rome, David. *Your Body Knows the Answer: Using Your Felt Sense to Solve Problems, Effect Change & Liberate Creativity.* Boston: Shambhala, 2014.

Roth, Gabrielle. *Maps to Ecstasy: A Healing Journey for the Untamed Spirit.* Novato, CA: Nataraj, 1998.

———. *Sweat Your Prayers: The Five Rhythms of the Soul.* New York: Penguin, 2005.

Rothschild, Babette. *The Body Remembers: The Psychophysiology of Trauma and Trauma Treatment.* New York: Norton, 2000.

———. *Help for the Helper: The Psychophysiology of Compassion Fatigue and Vicarious Trauma.* New York: Norton, 2006.

Rowan, John and Mick Cooper. *The Plural Self: Multiplicity in Everyday World,* London: Sage, 1999.

Rubenstein, Richard. *After Auschwitz: History, Theology, and Contemporary Judaism.* Second edition. Baltimore: Johns Hopkins University Press, 1992.

Ruether, Rosemary Radford. *Sexism and God-Talk: Toward a Feminist Theology.* Boston: Beacon, 1983.

Russell, Eileen. *Restoring Resilience: Discovering Your Clients' Capacity for Healing.* New York: Norton, 2015.

Russell, Letty. *The Future of Partnership.* Philadelphia: Westminster, 1979.

Sands, Kathleen. *Escape from Paradise: Evil and Tragedy in Feminist Theology.* Minneapolis: Fortress, 1994.

Schneider, Laurel. *Beyond Monotheism: A Theology of Multiplicity,* London: Routledge, 2008.

Schwarz, Hans. *Evil: A Historical and Theological Perspective.* Translated by Mark W. Worthing. Lima: Academic Renewal, 2001.

Schwartz, Richard. *Internal Family Systems.* New York: Guilford, 1997.

———. *You Are the One You've Been Waiting For: Bringing Courageous Love to Intimate Relationships.* Oak Park, IL: Trailheads, 2008.

Schweitzer, Don. *Contemporary Christologies: A Fortress Introduction.* Minneapolis: Fortress, 2010.

Shooter, Shelly. *How Survivors of Abuse Relate to God: The Authentic Spirituality of the Annihilated Soul.* Burlington, VT: Ashgate, 2012.

Simmons, Rachel. *Odd Girl Out: The Hidden Culture of Aggression in Girls.* New York: Harcourt, 2002.

Soelle, Dorothee. *Suffering.* Translated by Everett R. Kalin. Philadelphia: Fortress, 1975.

———. *The Strength of the Weak: Toward a Christian Feminist Identity.* Translated by Robert and Rita Kimber. Philadelphia: Westminster, 1984.

———. *Theology for Skeptics*. Translated by Joyce L. Irwin. Minneapolis: Fortress, 1995.

———. *Thinking About God: An Introduction to Theology*. Translated by John Bowden. Harrisburg, PA: Trinity, 1990.

———. *The Window of Vulnerability: A Political Spirituality*. Translated by Linda M. Maloney. Minneapolis: Fortress, 1990.

Solomon, Eldra, and Kathleen Heide. "The Biology of Trauma: Implications for Treatment." *Journal of Interpersonal Violence* 20 (2005) 51–60.

Spencer, Paul, ed. *Society and the Dance: The Social Anthropology of Process and Performance*. Cambridge: Cambridge University Press, 1985.

Steege, Mary. *The Spirit-Led Life: Christianity and the Internal Family System*. CreateSpace, 2010.

Suchocki, Marjorie Hewitt. *The End of Evil*. Albany: State University of New York, 1988.

———. *The Fall to Violence: Original Sin in Relational Theology*. New York: Continuum, 2004.

Sullender, R. Scott. "Vicarious Grieving and the Media." *Pastoral Psychology* 59 (2010) 191–200.

Swain, Storm. *Trauma and Transformation at Ground Zero*. Minneapolis: Fortress. 2011.

Sweezy, Martha, and Ellen Ziskind. *Innovations and Elaborations in Internal Family Systems Therapy*. New York: Routledge, 2017.

———. *Internal Family Systems Therapy: New Directions*. New York: Routledge, 2013.

Taylor, Mark C. *Erring: A Postmodern A/theology*. Chicago: University of Chicago Press, 1984.

Teicher, M. H., A. Tomoda, and S. L. Anderson. "Neurobiological Consequences of Early Stress and Childhood Maltreatment: Are Results from Human and Animal Studies Comparable?" *Annal of New York Academy of Science* (July 2006) 313–23.

Tessman, Lisa. *Burdened Virtues: Virtue Ethics for Liberatory Struggles*. New York: Oxford University Press, 2005.

Thistlethwaite, Susan Brooks, ed. *Adam, Eve, and the Genome: The Human Genome Project and Theology*. Minneapolis: Fortress, 2003.

Thistlethwaite, Susan Brooks. *Women's Bodies as Battlefield: Christian Theology and the Global War on Women*. New York: Palgrave Macmillan, 2015.

Thrift, Nigel. "The Still Point: Resistance, Expressive Embodiment and Dance." In *Geographies of Resistance*, edited by Steve Pile and Michael Keith. London: Routledge, 1997.

Tillich, Paul. "Paul Tillich in Conversation on Psychology and Theology." In *The Meaning of Health*, edited by Perry LeFevre. Chicago: Exploration, 1984.

———. *Dynamics of Faith*. New York: Harper & Row, 1958.

———. *Love, Power, and Justice*. London: Oxford University Press, 1954.

———. *Systematic Theology*. Volume 1. Chicago: University of Chicago Press, 1973.

———. *Systematic Theology*. Volume 2. Chicago: University of Chicago Press, 1975.

———. *Systematic Theology*. Volume 3. Chicago: University of Chicago Press, 1976.

Trible, Phyllis. *God and the Rhetoric and Sexuality*. Philadelphia: Fortress, 1978.

———. *Texts of Terror: Literary-Feminist Readings of Biblical Narratives*. Philadelphia: Fortress, 1984.

Turner, Leon. *Theology, Psychology and the Plural Self*. Burlington, VT: Ashgate, 2008.

Turner, Victor. *The Ritual Process: Structure and Anti-Structure*. New Brunswick: AldineTransaction, 2007.

Van der Hart, Onno, and Martin Dorahy. "History of the Concept of Dissociation." In *Dissociation and the Dissociative Disorders: DSM-V and Beyond,* edited by Paul Dell and John O'Neil. New York: Routledge, 2009.

Van der Kolk, Bessel. *The Body Keeps the Score: Brain, Mind, and Body in the Healing of Trauma.* New York: Viking, 2014.

Van Dernoot Lipsky, Laura, and Connie Burk. *Trauma Stewardship: An Everyday Guide to Caring for Self While Caring for Others.* San Francisco: Berrett-Koehler, 2009.

Van Gennep, Arnold. *The Rites of Passage.* Translated by M. Vizedom, and G. Caffee. Chicago: University of Chicago Press, 1960.

Watkins, John and Helen Watkins. *Ego States: Theory and Therapy,* New York: Norton, 1997.

Weaver, J. Denny. *The Nonviolent Atonement.* Grand Rapids: Eerdmans, 2001.

Weiss, Sandra. "Neurobiological Alterations Associated with Traumatic Stress." *Perspectives in Psychiatric Care* 43.3 (July 2007) 114–22.

West, Melissa Gayle. *Exploring the Labyrinth: A Guide for Healing and Spiritual Growth.* New York: Broadway, 2000.

Wiesel, Elie. *The Night Trilogy: Night, Dawn, Day.* New York: Hill and Wang, 2008.

Winton-Henry, Cynthia. *Dance—The Sacred Art: The Joy of Movement as a Spiritual Practice.* Woodstock: Skylight Paths, 2009.

Yehuda, Rachel, et. al. "Holocaust Exposure Induced Intergenerational Effects on FKBP5 Methylation." *Biological Psychiatry* 80 (2016) 372–80.

Zizioulas, John. *Communion & Otherness.* New York: T. & T. Clark, 2006.

Printed by Amazon Italia Logistica S.r.l.
Torrazza Piemonte (TO), Italy

11895245R00107